Praise for *If You Can Keep It*

"Everyone in every country, at every socioeconomic level, of every religious and secular persuasion, of every political bent, should read it. . . . It's the book you must read this year."

—Martha Rogers, PhD, coauthor of *Extreme Trust: Honesty as a Competitive Advantage*

"Eric Metaxas [is] one of our nation's most brilliant and morally serious public intellectuals."

—Robert P. George, McCormick Professor of Jurisprudence, Princeton University

"Irresistible . . . Compellingly written . . . Important. Not only should every American read it—they should then reread it aloud to their children and grandchildren."   —Dennis Prager

"Eric Metaxas has done a great service to the country."

—Gregory Alan Thornbury, PhD, president of the King's College, New York City

"A faith-based argument for American exceptionalism . . . that will appeal to Christian readers."   —*Kirkus Reviews*

ABOUT THE AUTHOR

Eric Metaxas is the #1 *New York Times* bestselling author of *Bonhoeffer: Pastor, Martyr, Prophet, Spy*; *Amazing Grace: William Wilberforce and the Heroic Campaign to End Slavery*; and *Miracles*. His books have been translated into more than twenty languages. His writing has appeared in *The Wall Street Journal*, *The New York Times*, and *The New Yorker*, and Metaxas has appeared as a cultural commentator on CNN, the Fox News Channel, and MSNBC. He is the host of *The Eric Metaxas Show*, a nationally syndicated daily radio show. Metaxas is also the founder and host of *Socrates in the City*, the acclaimed series of conversations on "life, God, and other small topics," featuring Malcolm Gladwell, Dick Cavett, and Rabbi Lord Jonathan Sacks, among many others. He is a senior fellow and lecturer at large at the King's College in New York City, where he lives with his wife and daughter.

www.ericmetaxas.com

 eric.metaxas

 @ericmetaxas

To Lindsey —

If You Can Keep It

THE FORGOTTEN PROMISE OF AMERICAN LIBERTY

Eric Metaxas

Eric Metaxas

PENGUIN BOOKS

PENGUIN BOOKS

An imprint of Penguin Random House LLC
375 Hudson Street
New York, New York 10014
penguin.com

First published in the United States of America by Viking Penguin,
an imprint of Penguin Random House LLC, 2016
Published in Penguin Books 2017

ISBN 9781101979983 (hardcover)
ISBN 9781101979990 (paperback)
ISBN 9781101980002 (ebook)

Printed in the United States of America
9   10   8

Set in Warnock Pro
Designed by Alissa Rose Theodor

This book is dedicated to my friend Os Guinness, for helping me see these inestimably important things

CONTENTS

If You Can Keep It

INTRODUCTION

The Promise

*Nothing is more wonderful than the art of
being free, but nothing is harder to learn
how to use than freedom.*

—Alexis de Tocqueville, *Democracy in America*

In the heart of Philadelphia, in a Georgian brick
building that still stands, one of the most extraordinary events in the history of the world took place. There, in
what is today called Independence Hall, over the course of about
one hundred days in the summer of 1787, some of the most
brilliant men of that or any other era created what would become the Constitution of a new country. They were creating the
legal foundation for a form of government that had never been

tried before; and they were creating the possibility—and the golden and glorious promise—of something called the United States of America.

The men in that room were an astounding array of the leading lights of American history. George Washington was there, along with Benjamin Franklin, James Madison, Alexander Hamilton, and Roger Sherman, among others. No one could reasonably debate whether the 4,200-word document they ended up with is one of the greatest documents in the history of the world. If its emergence there was not quite as unprecedented as Athena's parthenogenetic birth from the brow of Zeus, it is close enough to warrant comparison and amazement. The Constitution was a ship of state that the founders launched onto history's ocean that summer the likes of which had never before been seen. The world goggled at it. They also wondered: What would become of this great and strange bark? Would it sail long or soon sink? No one could know. And if it was to succeed and last, precisely how would it do that? How could it, being so very fragile? Why should it float for long? And yet it did. Whatever it was that they created that summer in that building has so grown and flourished in the more than two centuries following that it is simply without equal.

But who could know in 1787 what would spring from the nation made possible by that document created in those one hundred days? No one but God. Today we know that in historical terms, the nation there formed has since soared across the heavens like no other. But in 1787 it still only pointed toward the future, like an arrow in a cocked bow. The potential power in that bow was incalculable. But the promise of the arrow's flight had intrigued much of the world. It held great promise in many ways because it was itself a promise to every American, present and future, and to everyone in the world beyond America too.

In his famous "I Have a Dream" speech, Martin Luther King Jr. said that the Constitution and the Declaration of Independence before it constituted a "promissory note to which every American was to fall heir." It was a promise that was not fulfilled instantly and that was not fulfilled in King's day and that is not yet fulfilled in ours. At least not in full. It is a promise that is being fulfilled and that must keep on being fulfilled. And we are the ones who must fulfill it, who must keep that promise. But what is required of us to keep that promise and to continue to fulfill it?

What is required of us—of each one of us who are "we the people"—is something we have mostly forgotten. That is the reason I am writing this book. Benjamin Franklin sums all of this up in the title of this book, as I shall explain in a moment. But the main point is that each of us who call ourselves Americans has a great duty to keep that promise—and if we don't do our duty toward keeping that promise, our nation will soon cease to exist in any real sense. If that sounds overly dramatic, please keep reading.

It is not enough for us merely to exist as a people, doing the minimum of simply obeying our laws and minding our own business. Much more is required of Americans if America is truly to be America. In Dickens's *A Christmas Carol*, when Marley's ghost confronts Scrooge, Scrooge wonders at Marley's chains. What has his old business partner done to deserve such punishment? "But you were always a good man of business, Jacob," Scrooge says. To which Marley gives a forceful response: "Mankind was my business. The common welfare was my business; charity, mercy, forbearance, benevolence, were all my business. The dealings of my trade were but a drop of water in the comprehensive ocean of my business!"

Marley's bracing words might well suffice to sum up our situation as a nation. We cannot pretend that it's sufficient for us to mind our own business. The founders understood that the republic that came into being in 1787 could not continue long if every American did not make the business of that republic his or her business. They understood that America would not flourish without great help from all Americans. That was the only way it would work and the only way it could work. The government they had given us was something precious and fragile, a newborn babe for whom all of us were obliged to care. The ordered liberties and how they were to work together required a citizenry devoted to keeping them in order, so we were all in it together, else it would not work. So the promise of America in 1787 was a promise to all future Americans, as Dr.

King reminds us, as far into the future as we were willing to keep that promise. The possibility of our continuing to keep that promise would vanish if we failed to take our duties seriously. Future Americans depend on present-day Americans doing their duty in this. And there's even more to it than that. Because in the end the promise of this nation was also a promise to the whole world beyond this nation, as we shall see.

The Constitution given to us that 1787 was a sufficient beginning. It was the foundation of the United States of America, but merely existing—and merely obeying the laws that stem from that Constitution—was hardly what the founders had in mind. The idea that our government is "we the people" is not a corny idea that doesn't mean much. It is something that is utterly real. It is in fact an idea of great genius and is the main operating principle by which this nation has stayed alive and has expanded its freedoms for over two centuries. But once "we the people" begin to forget that, and cease to do what is necessary as Americans, it all begins to fall apart. And alas and alack, we have gone a long way toward forgetting that and toward ceasing to do what is necessary as Americans. We are in desperate, indeed urgent, need of a primer on these vital things.

On a lighter note, it may help to remember that in the movie *Annie Hall* Woody Allen says to Diane Keaton that a relationship is like a shark, and that in order to stay alive it must keep moving forward. "I think what we got on our hands," he says to her, "is a dead shark." So lest we become something similar, with infinitely greater consequences, we need to keep swimming. We can never say, "We have fulfilled the promise." It is an endless project, but continuing to fulfill that promise is at the very heart of what it means to be the United States of America. It is who we are. To cease doing what is necessary along these lines is to cease existing. But we are today in very real danger of doing just that, of becoming America in name only.

I believe our situation in present-day America is grave, but this book is not meant to be discouraging. In fact, by way of encouragement before we consider what we have forgotten and what we must do, let's first acknowledge that despite our difficulties and considerable failings, much of America's promise has already been fulfilled, and spectacularly so, far beyond what anyone might have imagined. For example, let's remember that the country created in that room in Philadelphia soon swelled westward to the mighty Mississippi and then crossed that divide to balloon farther westward to fill the entire continent, from one blue ocean to the other. Let's remember that eight decades after that summer the country would in the bloodletting of a terrible civil war legally cancel the shameful original sin of slavery. Let's remember that it would afterward create inventions unimaginable to previous generations, outracing sound via the telegraph and flooding silences with the music of the phonograph—and harnessing electricity to illuminate the darkness with delicate glass bulbs; and it would invent the motion picture so that people in darkened theaters could dream while still awake; and it would loft human beings into the world of the birds above our heads in winged apparatuses that would eventually soar across continents and then across oceans; and it would via assembly-line innovation make the horseless carriage available to the working man; and it would invent baseball and football and basketball; and it would in two wars defend civilization and democracy from totalitarian tyranny; and it would invent jazz and blues and rock and roll; and it would invent a device that could make what was happening in one place appear instantly to other people thousands of miles away; and it would make this device available to almost everyone; and it would vault our species beyond Earth's gravity and onto other heavenly bodies, depositing one, two, three, four, five, six, seven, eight, nine, ten, eleven, twelve men onto the white surface of the moon; and it would invent the computer and it would invent the Internet, with its endless information going to and fro over the surface of the Earth. All of these things and so many more were made possible by that one document written in that hot room in Philadelphia over the course of one hundred days—that promise to the future of the world.

But we must again remind ourselves that the Constitution guaranteed none of these future things, any more than the big bang or the cooling of the Earth guaranteed the Constitution. It was only a beginning that made them possible, just as it still makes so much more possible. The promise of that document has been kept to the extent that so much has been done thus far, but as I have said, it promises much more still to be kept, which must be kept now and tomorrow, by you and by me. And this vital idea that everything promised by the Constitution depended on the people of the newly formed country was not lost on those in that room in Philadelphia, as the following story makes clear.

"IF YOU CAN KEEP IT"

Dr. James McHenry, a delegate from Maryland, was at age thirty-four one of the youngest men at the convention. As things were breaking up at the end of the last day, McHenry was privileged to witness a historic exchange—and soon thereafter recorded it in his notes, which have survived. If not for his notes, we would have no record that this exchange ever happened. So what did the young doctor write? McHenry wrote that when Benjamin Franklin emerged from the building that day, he was accosted by a certain Mrs. Powell of Philadelphia. Whether she was a young woman or a dowager we don't know. He was then eighty-one years old, the oldest delegate, the éminence grise who for his part in those hallowed proceedings came to be known as the "sage of the Constitution." Franklin had by that time lived in Philadelphia sixty-four years since arriving there in 1723, aged seventeen, so for all we know, he knew this now-mythical and otherwise forgotten Mrs. Powell, who has come to stand for all of America since that day when she spoke to Franklin in a tone that seems to bespeak some degree of familiarity.

According to McHenry, Mrs. Powell put her question to Franklin directly: "Well, doctor," she asked him, "what have we got? A republic or a monarchy?"

Franklin, who was rarely short of words or wit, shot back: "A republic, madam—if you can keep it."

And there it was. But exactly what did Dr. Franklin mean by that?

One thing we know: What he meant was what we have been talking about and what everyone in the Constitutional Convention understood—that whatever document they ended up with, and whatever government it described and created, could be only a beginning. The people themselves would have to do a lot to make it work. A government in which the people would govern themselves would be fragile and would require the people's attention in a way that no other government would. If it had been a monarchy, or some other form of government with equally strong monarchic leanings—it would not have been up to the people to "keep" anything. The monarch or the powers of the monarchy would do all the "keeping" that was necessary and the role of "the people" would be nonexistent. But because what the founders created was a republic, the very opposite would be true. It would be we—"we the people," in the famous phrase—who must "keep" it.

So the Constitution was a pointer to something beyond itself, a promise, as I have said, one that could be broken or kept by the people to whom it was entrusted. There was no way that the words on the paper themselves could guarantee that anyone would abide by what they said, nor that the great promise of that document would be kept. By themselves the words were merely deaf, dumb, and mute shapes of inert black ink. What power did they have, lying there, to create a country, or to cause millions of people to behave in such a way that those people might flourish in future decades and centuries and might even bless others in other countries, exporting their ideas around the world? None. This, then, was the gamble of the founders—one that placed tremendous trust in the people to whom they bequeathed this fragile form of government. So the question must be *why* did they trust the people of the republic to keep the republic? The only answer to that question is that they knew the people of the American colonies at the end of the eighteenth century were prepared for the job of keeping it. Many factors had conspired to prepare them, to make them the perfect candidates to keep the republic entrusted to them, able to do what no one had ever done in the history of the world: to govern themselves. For one thing, they were the heirs of the tradition of British law, going all the way back to the Magna Carta in 1215. For another, because of the religious disparity among them they had a deep and abiding respect for religious freedom and were well practiced in living with those who held different beliefs from their own. And finally, because of their general religiousness many of them had a fealty to their faith communities that made them already likely to be governing themselves in ways that made the reigning governmental authority redundant. Thus they were uniquely prepared for this responsibility, and the founders could dream of entrusting it to them and did entrust it to them.

So by itself the Constitution could do very little. What it promised would require the efforts of all those who thenceforth called themselves Americans. It was they who must keep it, the republic and the grand and noble promise of that republic. That is the wonderful, spectacular genius of it all, and the terrible, sobering danger of it all too. The document and the men who created it put these unimaginably great and fragile things in the hands of the people. So these things—still unimaginably great and fragile—are in our hands now, this minute. We are ourselves this moment the keepers of the flame of liberty and the ones charged by Franklin and the other founders and by history past, present, and future with the keeping of this grand promise to the world.

If you are an American, you have tacitly agreed to join that group, to keep the republic Franklin spoke of that day. You might say that I've written this book to inform you of what you've gotten yourself into, because we really ought to know. In fact, if we haven't known about this, and most of us have not, there has been a profound disconnect in our relationship with our country. If we Americans cease to know that we are part of that group charged with the terrible and wonderful burden of keeping this glorious promise, the promise is already being broken and will soon be irrevocably so.

So Franklin's question is to you and to me: Can we keep it? And how?

KEEPING THE FLAME

Because the issue of whether we can keep the republic is so tremendously important, I wanted to frame it in another way, one that is very personal to me but that I think will help us all think about what it means to "keep" something, as Franklin said, and the implications of failing to keep it.

Almost every Easter since I was twelve, I've attended the midnight service at Assumption Greek Orthodox Church in Danbury, Connecticut, where I grew up. And every year, a few minutes before midnight, all of the lights in the church are put out and we stand there in the beautiful darkness, waiting and waiting. As we stand there in the holy silence and darkness, we are waiting for the light of the world. Then, finally, at the precise stroke of midnight, the priest shouts, *"Defte lavete Fos!"* Come receive the light! It is the great breaking of light into darkness, the advent of the resurrected Christ, the light of the eternal life of God now and forever quenching the darkness of eternal death. The priest in that moment lights his candle at the altar and with it then lights the candles of the altar boys, who go out into the congregation and light the candles of those in the first rows, who then turn around and light the candles of those behind them, who then turn around and light the candles of those behind them, on and on as the church gradually glows brighter and everyone in the quiet sanctuary lights his candle and then the candles of those around him. It is deeply beautiful and moving, something I look forward to and treasure every year. It is ancient and beautiful, a living symbol of light being shared in the holy darkness of the domed church, and a reprisal of the *"Fiat Lux!"* that was spoken by the creator at the beginning of time.

But even after this glorious moment, there is more. Because now comes the true practical challenge. With everyone's candles lit, the whole congregation follows the priest and the altar boys in a beautiful procession out of the church and around the whole church building. It is usually somewhat cold and windy and we must work hard to keep the flames of our candles from going out. Each candle has a small red chalicelike plastic cup that fits around the top, but that's often not enough to guard the flame from going out. After we have processed around the church, we gather at the foot of the church steps as the priest loudly proclaims, *"Christos Anesti!"*—Christ is risen!—and we join him, singing this anthem over and over, declaring it to the defeated darkness and all the while guarding our flames. After the service we all go to our cars and the driver hands his or her candle to a passenger and all the way home in the darkness, with almost no other cars on the road, we guard the flames. I've always wondered what our cars must look like to others out on the road at night, glowing from within with the light of two or more candles. When at two a.m. or later we arrive at the door of our home, we say a prayer and snuff the candle out by pushing it up against the door frame above our heads. Those black marks stay there year after year, reminding us of this tradition and of those prayers. But unless we have kept the flame lit all the way home, we cannot experience this special moment when we say our prayer as we put the candle out against the doorjamb. Only then is our job done, and we take it very seriously.

I remember all of this now because what the founders gave us is like that flame. There is something holy about it, but once they passed it to us, their job was done. They could only hope and pray that we would guard it and tend it and keep it, so that it wouldn't go out. That flame was passed from them to others, who passed it to others, who passed it to others—and it is at this moment in history in our hands, yours and mine. The burden of "keeping it," as Franklin said, is excruciatingly important. And here is the main reason for that: Once it goes out, it goes out forever. If the flame given to us goes out, we not only lose the light ourselves forever but will also lose the ability to pass it along to all those others who are waiting for it. That is what makes keeping it so important and the thought of letting it go out so terrible and tragic.

For reasons I shall explain in the course of this book, I'm

afraid we are in serious danger of letting it go out in our generation. So it is genuinely urgent that we understand where we are and that we do all we can to make sure that we do not let this flame of ordered liberty given to us by the founders go out. We must do it not just for our own sake but also for the sake of all those waiting for us to light their candles, so to speak. We must do what we can to see what we have been given and to do what is expected of us. We have a charge to keep. This book is about seeing that we understand this again—and that we keep that charge, that republic, that glorious promise.

ONE

The Idea of America

There was in the beginning a wildness to America, and perhaps it was that aspect of this new land that enabled those settling here to have ideas that bore the stamp of that native wildness. Because the experiment in liberty called America was and remains a genuinely wild idea, something that ought to be arresting when we see it, and perhaps a bit shocking too. It's not something easily or intuitively grasped, the way one grasps the infinitely cruder idea that "might makes right," and that if someone more powerful than you decides to rule over you, you have few choices and had probably better comply. If we are to "keep" this republic, we have to see it afresh and really understand what we're keeping, must have a clear grasp of what this American republic is and how it works. Let's go back to the beginning, to when America was newly born, when those present at her birth couldn't help but see how extraordinary and precious and wild an idea she was.

In 1776 a nation was formed in a way that a nation never had been formed. It was something entirely new: *the nation as idea.* For the first time, a nation was created that was not merely a group of ethnically or tribally similar people. Nor was it a nation composed of disparate groups held together by a strong leader. Until the advent of the United States of America, these were the two groups into which nations must fall. There was no other option or category. Most countries fell into the first category because every Frenchman or German or Greek or Japanese knew that his country was made up of others similar to him in ethnic makeup, language, and culture. Anyone who did not share these things was a foreigner.

In the second category we may place all empires, such as those of Alexander the Great and of the Romans—and the British Empire and, in more recent times, the Iraq of Saddam Hussein, which was a nation of Shia Arabs, Sunni Arabs, and Kurds who, but for the brutal peace kept by their strongman dictator, would have been at war with one another.

The country born in 1776, however, fit neither of these categories, standing quite apart in the history of nations and peoples. But what was it exactly—and where had it come from? It was a nation held together by an idea and by citizens who bought into that idea. They were of different backgrounds and different religions. Some of them lived in Maine and others in Virginia and others in Georgia—and others in all the colonies in between. But they all were Americans because they voluntarily believed in that idea. That a nation could be held together by people believing in an idea was unprecedented, as I have said. It had never happened before and has really never happened again. It was nothing more and nothing less than this singular idea that held America and Americans together, and the idea in which they believed was, in a word, *liberty*.

But the strangeness and foreignness of this new nation "conceived in liberty" is simply impossible to appreciate fully today. One major reason for this is that the United States and the idea—or the set of ideas—that came together to create it have been so successful that they've been copied endlessly in the two-plus centuries since. Today there are many nations around the world that, while not quite like the United States, nonetheless resemble her in one way or another. So the United States simply doesn't look unique as it once did. The freedoms that we alone had in 1776 are now freedoms that are enjoyed by the citizens of many countries around the world. We might say that in this aspect we are the victims of our own success, and of course we should be deliriously happy so to be. It is a testimony to the triumph of the ideas that led to our founding and that saw us through these two centuries of magnificent and world-changing accomplishments. But back in 1776 and in the decades after, this nation was all alone in embodying these ideas, so it was very easy to see them clearly. Its uniqueness at that time can hardly be overstated. It was as if in a vast field of daisies a sunflower suddenly sprang up to tower and totter above all the others, strange and alone. What was it? And how had it gotten there?

To be sure, the world hardly knew what to make of it, although some around the world were cheering us on. They saw that we were onto something that was new in history, and the idea that we were putting our ideas about liberty into actual practice was exhilarating to watch. Still, they couldn't help but wonder whether the experiment would last. Whether it *could*. Surely it must topple soon enough! The similar ideas that erupted in France and led to the French Revolution ended in a grotesque bloodbath. Would America follow suit? No one knew. So over its first years and decades the world watched this new nation and marveled at it. What should they make of this huge and ungainly and curious thing? Some honest observers saw that, like that sunflower, it was a bit raw and oversized. It was not as genteel as the other flowers. It was so big and growing so fast that it was a bit clumsy and uncomfortable standing there. But there was something cheerful and young about it too. America stood there alone, raw-boned and grinning at the world around her. Where had she come from and what would become of her?

That's the question: Can we behold ourselves afresh, as we did in the beginning? Because unless we can do that, we cannot understand the ideas that brought us into being and allowed us to continue all these years. Unless we can see what brought us into existence, we cannot understand what so many other countries emulated in their various ways and degrees of success. It's our job to "keep" the republic called America, and we can hardly keep what we don't even know we have. So what is the secret of our success? You might simply call it the idea of American liberty, which might also simply be called self-government.

But first let's say a word about something else. In a way it is this more than anything that makes us "exceptional": the idea that America exists primarily not for itself but for others. This is a strange idea, and easily misunderstood, so we should take a moment to clarify what it means.

A NATION FOR OTHERS

There's a paradox at the center of what's been called American exceptionalism. It's that a significant part of what makes us exceptional is that in some sense we are a nation with a mission beyond ourselves and beyond our borders. We are a nation with a mission to the rest of the world. This idea is startling but inescapable. If we are to keep the republic, then, our keeping it is not merely for our own sake. This is a big idea, not often heard.

And it can be stretched in the wrong direction. But at its core it is true and extremely important.

One image that is central to who we are is the Statue of Liberty. We will, of course, remember that she is facing outward and that she is carrying a torch and holding it high. She does this for others. She wants them to see her and to make their way toward her, toward liberty. She is something like a copper-sheathed literalization of John Winthrop's "City upon a Hill"—shining for the world to see, as an example, as if to say, *You can come here and we will welcome you and you can do what we are doing. You can participate in this. This is not just for us. It's meant for you too. In fact, the only reason we have it is so that we can share it with you.*

And this has happened to a great extent. Many have come to our shores and become Americans. And many have taken our ideas back to their parts of the world, as intended. I've said that it's a testimony to America that the ideas we alone embodied at our beginning have been exported to many nations around the world, and this quality—one might even call it a kind of generosity—has much to do with our success. Ronald Reagan had a plaque on his desk that said "There is no limit to what a man can do or where he can go if he does not mind who gets the credit." In a way, that principle has been at work in how America has shared what is best about it. So today the very ideas that made us exceptional at our beginning are present throughout much of the rest of the world and no longer recognized as having originated here. This is a testimony to the power of those ideas, and it is a testimony to the idea that these ideas were from the beginning and still are meant not to be kept for ourselves but to be exported, to be shared for the benefit of the whole world.

It's an interesting thing that we have not copyrighted our ideas about liberty or tried to charge others to use them, or even to credit us when they do so. We've given these ideas away freely. To what end? We have not calculated the benefit to ourselves much. Some have said that we do what we do for purely selfish or mercenary reasons, that we fought in Iraq, for example, because of our oil interests. Such views are not only deeply cynical but also fail to account for much else that we do. Are we being self-serving in what we've done in Africa to combat AIDS? Are we being self-serving in sending ships and supplies to disaster areas around the world? Unless we are hopelessly bound by cynicism, we have to acknowledge that the United States has been remarkably and consistently generous in sharing what it has, whether material things or ideas.

We really have demonstrated our belief in the idea that if we bless others, we will be blessed. It's the "rising tide lifts all boats" philosophy first popularized by John F. Kennedy. We've believed that if we help others it will come back to us, and we haven't done that in a calculating way. There is something in the American cultural character that is simply like this, that believes this is the right way to conduct ourselves.

It was from the beginning at the center of our purpose in history to share whatever goodness with which God had blessed us. We have opened our borders to the immigrant. We have exported our ideas about liberty—about human rights and human dignity and about free markets and religious freedom—across the vast globe. The West is filled with ideas that were born in the cradle of America. These ideas that a nation should care for its poor, that the wealthy—via taxes or via the private sector or both—should help to lift up those who cannot lift themselves, is now taken for granted in the civilized West. Who today would dare say that the poor should look after themselves and that no one bears any responsibility to help them?

If we once stood out like a sunflower in a field of daisies, we are today surrounded by many other sunflowers of varying types, and perhaps even a few sunflower-daisy hybrids, to push the metaphor. It is now difficult to see what we looked like in the beginning, when we were the only sunflower in the field. But as I have said, that is all to the good. It speaks to the unprecedented success of the American experiment.

Let's also be clear that the founders—and certainly many protofounders, such as Massachusetts Bay governor John Winthrop—explicitly understood this idea that what we had was meant not just for us but for the rest of the world. As I have said, we have in large part succeeded in sharing it. As I have also said, by making us look less strange and singular, it is harder for us to see ourselves clearly, to see what it was that made us different in the beginning. And it is precisely that which we must "keep."

Therefore, if in any sense we care about the rest of the world, we must first "keep" this republic. We are to shine not so that we can admire our own brightness but so that we hold out a beacon of hope to the rest of the world. Our exceptionalness is not for us *but for others*. That is the paradox at the heart of who we are. So what makes us different has nothing to do with jingoism and nationalistic chest beating. If we have ever been great, it is only because we have been good. If we have ever been great, it is only because we have longed to help make others great too. That earnest humility and generosity must be attended to.

We therefore must apprehend the idea that if we cease to be strong—and if we cease to be the America we were at first—the whole world will suffer. So if for no other reason than that, we must care about America. It is like the woman who says, "I must stay healthy for the sake of my children. They need me." This might strike some as paternalistic, or in this case perhaps maternalistic, but what if there is truth in it? And there is.

Which takes us back to Franklin's words to Mrs. Powell that day in Philadelphia. When he asked whether we could keep the republic entrusted to us, what was it exactly that he thought needed keeping? That's what we've got to see and understand once more.

THE FORGOTTEN MIRACLE OF SELF-GOVERNMENT

Most of us don't understand the idea of self-government enough to be properly astonished by it. But in the day of our nation's birth the idea of self-government was so new as to be staggering. In fact, it was shocking even to some Americans, who during the revolution simply rejected it, choosing instead to side with the British Crown as Tories. All of the great nations of Europe had been ruled by monarchs since time immemorial. For many the idea of detaching from something that had been stable and continuous for many centuries seemed like uncharted lunacy. Everyone understood that some monarchs were more benevolent than others, and that some nations enjoyed more freedom than others, but nowhere on the globe was there a nation that had come near to throwing away the very idea of monarchy and declaring, "We will have no government but the people themselves." It was a decidedly radical notion, if not a preposterous one.

So to anyone at that time—but to us too, who have forgotten about this—it was logical to ask the question: Precisely how could "the people" govern? After all, when in the history of the modern world had anyone entrusted its government to the people? One had to look all the way back to antiquity, to ancient Greece, twenty long centuries earlier, to see anything at all similar. But the democracies of ancient Greece, while certainly serving as encouragements and inspirations to the founders, were nonetheless different in important ways. For one thing, they were far smaller, involving only very small city-states. And Athens—the best and largest of these—could not sustain anything like real democracy for very long. Already in the fourth century BC, when Alexander the Great marched onto the scene, democracy in ancient Greece was over. So the democracies of ancient Greece were only dim, hopeful flickerings of the bright flame that would burst into existence in 1776, when two and a half million people in a vast area stretching from Maine to Georgia would be united in one government as a single, sovereign nation, alone on the edge of a wild and endless continent. Why in the world did the founders think it would work?

THE NECESSITY OF GOVERNMENT

Before we answer that question and sing the praises of American independence and American freedom and self-government, let's remind ourselves that any reasonably good government— including a monarchy—is far better than no government. Infinitely so. To have no government at all simply means anarchy;

and where there is anarchy the strong will soon oppress the weak, usually cruelly. Anyone who has seen human beings brutalized by other human beings knows that there is an important role for government. On the simplest level, government exists to protect innocent people: both from within, from those who would steal and rape and murder; and from without, from foreign powers that would do the same on a wider scale. In order to deal with the passions of fallen human beings, some government is therefore necessary. Throughout history people have known that if someone stepped out of line, a sword—literal or figurative—would stop them. Thus it was the sword of government that in every culture and society defined the limits of how one could behave, and considering the possibilities for oppression, it was usually a good thing, relatively speaking.

If mankind had always required the "sword of government" to keep certain troublemakers from destroying all order, just how was the founders' idea of freedom supposed to work? What did it mean to say that this thing called "freedom" could coexist with government? How could this group at the end of the eighteenth century suppose they would accomplish this? Precisely how would their freedom be different from mere anarchy? And even if such freedom could somehow be achieved within the context of a government, how could it possibly be sustained?

Wouldn't anything like real freedom be tremendously fragile and therefore short-lived?

WHAT IS AMERICAN FREEDOM?

American freedom is, of course, nothing like pure and unmitigated freedom—which would indeed be anarchy and no freedom at all. True freedom must be an "ordered freedom," at the center of which is what we call "self-government." So to be clear: People would not have freedom from government, but would have freedom from *tyrannous* government, or from government that might easily *become* tyrannous. The ordered freedom given to us by the founders was meant to enable the people to govern themselves. But again, what made the framers think they could buck a trend extending back into the swamps of prehistory? How did they think they could create something so categorically different from anything that had ever existed?

Here was the conundrum: Though people needed some kind of government to keep them from killing one another or stealing from one another or brutally subjugating one another, "government" was often no more than the strongest warrior or group of warriors taking over and imposing their will. Often they had risen to "govern" in the most violent fashion and governed that way as well. They did not so much govern as rule. So the top warrior would be called the king, but his resemblance to such monarchs as Louis XIV or Queen Victoria was, as it were, minimal. In such cases one was inevitably dependent on the benevolence of whoever ruled, and one's whole life—the shape and quality of it—depended on the character of that ruler, who had either risen in brutal fashion or who had inherited rulership from someone who had risen that way.

Now and again a group might overthrow that brutal ruler, but then that second group would rule and a new ruler would emerge. Even if the peasants were to rise up in a rebellion against their king, the peasants would have a leader. If their rebellion were successful, that leader would rise to rule and his character would define the lives of all under him. No one in the history of the world had ever conceived of the idea that there could be a rebellion against a leader that would end *not* in a new leader but in a new kind of leadership altogether—a leadership that was accountable to those whom it led. This, as I have said, was a new idea in the history of the world. Where had it come from?

The founders had studied history and found themselves at a particular moment when circumstances allowed history to change forever, as though it had been plodding along in two dimensions and suddenly it was possible to burst into a third. It was a singular moment in the history of the world. We so take self-government for granted in our time that it is almost impossible for us to behold the utter foreignness of it in its day, to see the astonishing and startling nature of its birth in history.

The founders were brilliant men with a remarkable sense of history, so they were particularly sensitive to the unprecedented strangeness of it all. They understood that for an idea as wild as theirs to do more than burst onto the scene and then disappear again would take tremendous forethought and planning. They knew that the revolt against England was only the first step. That revolution was itself nearly impossible. As I have said, there had been other revolutions and uprisings in history whereby one ruler or group of rulers replaced another. But the founders knew that if they won the war they had another impossible obstacle ahead: creating a government in which the people could rule themselves. If it had never been done before, why did they think it could be done now?

HOW DOES SELF-GOVERNMENT WORK?

The founders understood that for people to govern themselves, two things that had never before existed must be brought into existence simultaneously. The first had never existed in the unadulterated form in which it would exist now; and the second had really never existed at all. Both spoke to an understanding of mankind that was corroborated by observation and history and that was, in the founders' estimation, a biblical understanding of things. Each of the two things answered a particular question and solved a particular problem: The first understood that man was fallen, and the second understood that he could be redeemed.

The first of the two things was simply the structure of the government. A view of mankind as fallen meant that a government must be created that took this into account and whose very structure limited the power of any one part, lest that power grow and take over, devolving into tyranny. It was an observable fact of history that everyone wanted power and more power. If people had no power they wanted to get it, and if someone had power he wanted to keep it—and if possible to get more of it. So the founders must create a government that somehow took this into account, that was structured so that this fallen and selfish human desire for power actually *worked against itself.*

Of course, most of us know this as the ideas of democracy and checks and balances. The founders came to the idea of checks and balances mainly through the writings of John Locke and Montesquieu, and to the idea of democracy through the ancient Greeks and Romans. But who would believe that the citizens of those ancient societies were truly free? Rome was more an oligarchy than a true democracy, and it was a brutal society where being out of step with those in power could bring swift and cruel death. And Greece was the place where Socrates had been forced to drink a cup of poison for openly questioning the gods and ideas of that culture. If one's thoughts were regulated by the power of the state, how could one really be free?

The founders would take the best of these ideas and improve upon them in some revolutionary ways to create the freest country that had ever existed—and more than that, the freest people. But again, what did they propose that was different from what had gone before? How could they safely give citizens a far greater freedom than anyone had ever enjoyed? Their success lay mainly in the second thing, which was unprecedented.

This second piece was the secret ingredient, really, because it was not something that could be created in the way that a system of government could be created. It was infinitely more difficult than drafting a system of checks and balances. No, this second thing must already exist. And this second thing was the answer to the question of questions: *What would enable a group of people to be trusted to govern themselves and then actually to do so?*

Because one had to ask: If you enabled people to pick their own leaders, what would prevent them simply from voting for their friends, or for those who would favor them over others? Why wouldn't they simply vote to line their own pockets or choose leaders who would give them what they wanted at the expense of what was right for everyone? Why wouldn't they use this system to steal from the national treasury? In short, given the lesson of history that human beings were selfish and desirous of power, why should the founders assume that true self-government could ever work? The answer, as we have said, lies in the second thing. And that thing was, in a word, *religion*.

EACH PERSON MUST GOVERN HIMSELF

To begin with, we must make clear that "religion" as the founders understood it was dramatically different from religion as it had been understood in other societies; in fact, we may well prefer the term "free religion" to simple "religion." Because in America the idea of religious freedom was paramount. It was always understood that one's religion was truly free, which is to say not coerced nor mandatory nor affiliated with the power of the state in any way. This was also unprecedented.

The idea that religion was valuable in keeping people from misbehaving was not lost on rulers throughout history. Some rulers were tyrants who merely used state power to crush dissent and misbehavior and lawlessness, but other rulers cannily and often cynically understood that religion could help them to rule. They knew that religious people were less likely to misbehave. But the people were never free to believe as they liked. They were forced to go to church and bow to the ecclesiastical authorities just as they were forced to pay taxes or tribute and bow to the king. They did not have freedom of religion. There was one state church and the people must attend it and bow to its authority just as they bowed to the authority of the state. Indeed, the authority of the church and the authority of the state were in many situations precisely the same authority. Religion had been used to oppress people just as state authority had been used to oppress people. In the nineteenth century Karl Marx famously called religion "the opiate of the masses," and regarding this kind of religion there is in fact great truth to his statement.

The founders, however, had quite another idea, based on their experience in the colonies over the decades before, where actual religious freedom had existed. They had already experienced this religious freedom as part of life in the American colonies. Some of the very first settlers on American shores had left their lives behind precisely for this freedom. So the founders had observed something entirely different in America, something that had successfully operated for nearly a century: the tolerance of other denominations and religions, such that the people were not coerced to believe but could believe and worship precisely as they wished.

They knew that the religion that was necessary to self-government was not coerced but free. True religion must be free religion. This was something new, and this was what made possible the unprecedented experiment in liberty that came to be known as the United States of America.

So the founders understood that freedom and religion went

hand in hand, that freedom must have religion and religion must have freedom. One without the other was in fact neither. Freedom without religion would devolve into license or end in tyranny; and religion without freedom would really be only another expression of tyranny. The challenge was to combine them. Somehow.

So yes, there was something called the social contract, where we each give up something to the community—surrender certain freedoms and pay taxes to a government so that the laws can be enforced. And yes, there was something called the law that would enforce the social contract, and there was a document called the Constitution that would be the basis of those laws. But the founders understood that what they had in mind had to be much more than these things. What was required was a virtuous people who were prepared to handle the great freedom being proposed. And the founders saw an extraordinary opportunity—one that had never existed before in history. As we will see in chapter 3, what George Whitefield and the Great Awakening would make possible was now in 1776 ready to be tested. A people had been prepared to do something never done before, to govern themselves. In many ways they had been governing themselves already. But now the training wheels of the British monarchy would need to be removed. They would see whether they could ride the bicycle by themselves, or whether they would crash. The founders understood that the more each person governed himself, the less there would be a need for strong government, and by their estimation the American people were ready. The faith and the virtue of the American people made possible the most free nation in the history of the world.

Precisely how all the elements would work together we will consider in more depth in the next chapter, in which I explain the "Golden Triangle of Freedom," a brilliant concept put forward by the cultural and political observer Os Guinness in his important book, *A Free People's Suicide*. The term "Golden Triangle of Freedom" is his own coinage, as is his excellent explanation of it in that book, but the dynamic described was understood by the founders, who would rely on it in the government they were creating. Another reason I wanted to write this book was that I had never heard about these things growing up and I realized that several generations of Americans have missed these seminal ideas as well.

The founders likely took the dynamic of the Golden Triangle at least somewhat for granted, because so much of it was already woven into the fabric of the society and culture in which they lived. It seems that because of this they did not take as many pains to explain it as they might have done. But it well describes the secret at the heart of the success of America. In a way, the Golden Triangle of Freedom is the engine that has enabled us to be the freest people in the history of the world for more than two centuries, and if we would continue so to be, if we would "keep" the republic entrusted to us, we must refamiliarize ourselves with this. The Golden Triangle of Freedom beautifully encapsulates the delicate and dynamic way that freedom and faith actually sustain each other.

Before we launch into that chapter, we should expand for a moment on what American freedom is *not*. Let's briefly look at something tremendously important to the larger conversation, something we may call "the limits of freedom."

THE LIMITS OF FREEDOM

The idea of freedom can be misunderstood in a variety of ways, but for our purposes let's point out the two principal ones: what we may call the "liberal" misunderstanding and the "conservative" misunderstanding.

The "liberal" misunderstanding of American freedom, in short, is when freedom—or liberty—is confused with license. License to do anything at any time is not what the founders had in mind when they were talking about freedom. The difference between these two concepts was illustrated most pointedly immediately after the terrible events of September 11, 2001. As a way of making sense of why we had been attacked, it was often said that the terrorists simply "hated our way of life"—that they hated freedom itself. But what exactly was it about our "way of life" and our "freedom" that they hated? To be sure, one American's way of life and ideas about freedom are not always the same as another American's.

Not long after 9/11, a panelist on a major talk show expressed genuine anger at the Taliban and those who had attacked the United States. She said that as a response to their terrorist attacks, she wished our American planes would drop blow-up sex dolls and Pamela Anderson videos over the Taliban. As if that would send the necessary message to those oppressive Muslim fundamentalists! It would show them! As far as she was concerned, that would hit those bearded patriarchal bigots where they lived. She seemed to think that American freedom was principally about having no sexual limits, about the throwing off of all "oppression" and, most important, sexual oppression—or repression. It was a classically Freudian idea of the problem at the center of human life, and as far as she was concerned, that was what our American freedom existed to wipe out.

This suggestion that raining pornography and sex toys might pointedly express American freedom was an important and bracing moment in television history, because the divide between the founders' view of "liberty" and the current misunderstanding of it had never been more perfectly contrasted. But what had happened in the centuries since the ideas based on Montesquieu and Locke and Jesus had devolved into what amounted to an airdropped candygram for Mongo to the medieval coelacanths in their Afghani caves? During previous wars we might have thought to drop Bibles or copies of our Constitution, because we knew that these contained the ideological dynamite to free these cultures of their oppressive bindings. Indeed, in some cases we had done things along these lines. But by the time of this panelist's exclamations those ideas had been for the most part lost to American culture—and certainly to the cultural "thought leaders" in places like the mainstream networks. For them—and for many in their television audience— liberty had become mere licentiousness and leering license. In fact, for these people in their Manhattan media bubble, so deeply out of touch with middle America, anyone advocating the moral code of the Bible was only one step away from the bearded members of the Taliban.

But now let's look at the "conservative" misunderstanding of freedom, which was also perfectly illustrated during the time following 9/11. On the opposite side of the ideological divide from the panelist and many in the so-called mainstream media stood President George W. Bush and the people in his cabinet at that time, such as Dick Cheney and Donald Rumsfeld. The political ideology that sums up their way of approaching things has been termed *neoconservatism*. And the particular flaws in that ideology were illuminated as these neoconservatives began to formulate a way to fight back against those who had attacked us.

To remind ourselves, our first enemy at that time was the Taliban, a tremendously repressive Muslim group that had taken over Afghanistan and that had created a safe haven for the terror group Al Qaeda, which had attacked us. We believed the Taliban— known to be religiously fundamentalist in the extreme—must be rooted out of Afghanistan so that terrorist groups there would not be given safe haven, a place from which to conduct their evil campaigns. Our second enemy ended up being the regime of the Iraqi dictator Saddam Hussein, whom nearly everyone—including Hillary Clinton and other top Democrats—strongly suspected of possessing weapons of mass destruction, which might easily fall into the hands of Al Qaeda. Much ink has been spilled on these two subjects, but for our purposes here let's simply focus on what the Bush administration seemed to think would happen in Afghanistan and Iraq once our troops had freed the peoples there—from the Taliban on the one hand and from Saddam Hussein on the other.

The false "conservative" hope was that American-style "freedom" would erupt just as soon as the people of Afghanistan were freed from the repressive Taliban and as soon as the Iraqis were freed from Saddam Hussein. It was as if we needed only to remove the shackles and they would all leap up and commence self-government, as if they were only waiting to don tricorn hats and pen fiery pamphlets against the tyrannous perfidy of King George III. President Bush repeatedly spoke about how freedom is mankind's natural condition, stating that it is a gift from God to everyone in the world. There is great truth to this, of course. But alas, there's more to it—much more. Indeed, without that "much more" it simply cannot work. It's not a mere matter of removing shackles or oppressive governments. Newborn colts can walk as soon as they are born, but when it comes to self-government, human beings are more like newborn humans, for whom walking takes a long time. We need to be babied and cared for before we are able to do things like walk or feed ourselves.

The point is that there is so much that needs to be in place to make what we call freedom and self-government work than to simply tell someone he is free and bid him govern himself is like saying because of the Second Amendment we could hand out loaded guns to children. There are tremendous responsibilities that come with self-government, as I shall explain, and it took the American people a very long time to get ready for 1776. The idea that American freedom and democracy and self-government simply amount to being able to vote is false. So the ubiquitous pictures of Afghan women with purpled thumbs were indeed encouraging and inspiring, but if we thought those ink-stained fingers had overnight turned these women into Abigail Adams or Martha Washington, we were sorely mistaken and in the last ten-plus years have been shown to be so. Merely being able to vote is a great yawning abyss away from being able to govern oneself, an abyss whose size may be partially measured in the blood and treasure spent there in the years since. This misunderstanding of American liberty is no small misunderstanding.

This idea that "democratic" voting is all that's necessary for freedom and self-government has been demonstrated many times to be false. In Germany in the 1930s the people "freely" elected a government that would eventually do all it could to destroy their freedoms, using the "democratic" process along the way. It is quite possible for people to democratically elect someone who is an enemy of freedom. And not only that, but the people in the voting booths can themselves be culpable.

For example, we understand that to some extent people vote for their self-interests; that's part of how voting is supposed to work. But voting purely for one's self-interest can work against freedom. Someone might want to vote for a person he knows as a friend, but what if he knows that the policies of his friend's opponent would actually be better for the country? Or what if we know a candidate's policies will help us personally but in the end will harm the country? Don't we as voters bear a serious responsibility to think about the whole country and about its future? We have to voluntarily balance that weighty responsibility with pure self-interest. But in a democracy no one can force us to take that larger responsibility seriously. There are many examples where citizens have not taken it seriously and have voted in such a way that may have benefited them in the short term but which harmed the country—and often themselves and their children and grandchildren—in the long term.

These kinds of abuses of democracy can happen in a number of ways and always lead the nation away from democracy. For democracy to truly work, not just for one or two elections but for dozens and for hundreds, requires much more than people merely voting. The ordered liberties given to us by the founders work together as part of a fragile mechanism. People must understand that their responsibilities as citizens are so serious as to be vital to the democracy itself. If the voter is not voluntarily selfless to some extent, and does not merely think of himself but of others; and if he does not think just about the present, but about the future, it all falls apart over time. Self-government will not work unless the citizens bear the responsibility to vote in such a way that continues their freedoms and their ability to have free elections, that continues their economic prosperity. They have to vote in a way that does not trade the future for the present.

This "conservative" misunderstanding of freedom is closely linked to the false idea that the free market will by itself magically lead to all kinds of freedoms, which is similarly misguided. This is not to say that the free market is not a good thing, or to say that it cannot take a society a long way in the direction of other kinds of freedoms. But there are some who seem to think that the free market can never fail to lead a society the whole way. But if you look at how the "invisible hand of the market" works, you will see that this is not possible. The free market is amoral. It delivers what people want, so if the desires of the people are good desires, good things will come. But if people want better and cheaper pornography and better and cheaper drugs, the free market will oblige. It has no moral compunctions about doing so. If people want what is good, the market will deliver that, but no one can force them to "want" what is good.

Neither in voting nor in finance is pure self-interest always in the best interest of the nation. You may recall Michael Douglas's character's infamous statement in the movie *Wall Street*. With his slicked-back hair, Gordon Gekko declared, "Greed is good." In fact it is not. It's not only not good, it is evil. But it is not only evil and morally wrong, it will in the end lead to the debasement and destruction of the free market, just as naked and selfish self-interest in voting will lead to the debasement and destruction of democratic self-government.

And as I have said, the government cannot force us to be "good" or "moral" or "selfless." The Constitution simply doesn't have that power. But if being good and moral and selfless is necessary for our form of government to work properly over the long run, and if the founders understood that, how is it supposed to happen?

THE GOVERNMENT CANNOT FORCE US TO BE GOOD

The free market can be corrupted. When the people running the stock exchanges discover that they can bake rules into the system that allow them to take advantage of tiny loopholes no one else could ever hope to have the time or attention to be aware of, they are "legally" gaming the system. No amount of regulation can ever deal with this. Other "legal" loopholes will be found and we will end where we began. But how to solve that problem? The government is powerless to solve it, and if it tries, it often only makes the problem worse. If it is to be solved, it must be the people—and the culture—that solves the problem.

So it's not the role of the government to solve all of our problems through legislation. Some problems cannot be cured through legislation. But they must be attended to nonetheless. And here's the problem: The less the culture attends to these things, the more the government will attend to them and the less freedom there will be. The greater the role the government plays, the more it crowds out the culture's role, the role of the people—and the true freedom of the people.

The people must guard this freedom, must use it or lose it, as the saying goes. To the extent that we are not using it, we are indeed losing it—and will lose it forever, as the cultural muscles atrophy and atrophy further.

To use a grim example by way of illustration, in Saddam Hussein's Iraq there was no need for people to govern themselves. The governmental power of Saddam Hussein's tyranny was so crushing and so brutal that whatever muscles once existed in the Iraqi people to think for themselves and govern themselves had over the course of decades atrophied to nothing. It is as if one were to put on an Iron Man suit that moves one's arms and legs—a kind of exoskeleton that does what we should do. In time, our muscles will grow so weak that if you remove the suit, you have a person underneath who is so weak he won't be able to walk or lift an arm. Anyone over a certain age who has been laid up in a hospital bed knows how real this can be. It can take a very long time in rehab to get the muscles back to do the most basic things. It cannot happen overnight. With Iraq, it was as if the United States took off the Iron Man suit and told the Iraqi people, "Okay, you're free! You're free to run and leap! Go!" But they could barely stand, much less walk or run. They hadn't used those muscles in many decades. It would take a long time to see whether they could ever run or leap. Fifteen years after we took off their Iron Man suit, it's clear we miscalculated things rather badly.

A similar thing happened in Russia. Many conservatives believed that all that was necessary was to remove the communist dictatorship and *voilà*, the people of Russia would become just like us. But for seventy years they had not been educated in how to govern themselves. They had none of what Alexis de Tocqueville has called the "habits of the heart" that were in place in the United States when it began its own existence. So they have elected Vladimir Putin, who is hardly a friend to what we think of as freedom. That they elected him "democratically" is beside the point. That they have a "free market" economic system now, which they didn't have for seventy years, is also largely beside the point. Their system is corrupt, and many have cynically made peace with that corruption, because anything else is simply unknown to them. They feel that they must simply play the game and try to win, but to think about noble ideas like self-government and a free market that blesses others is rightly thought a luxury they cannot afford.

If you take God and faith and morality out of the equation, everything inevitably falls apart. It cannot be otherwise. The Russian people in 1991 and the people of Iraq in 2002 had not been properly prepared for the great responsibilities of their newfound freedoms. That they are not nearly where we might have hoped they might be today illustrates this tragically. Freedom is delicate and fragile. In the wrong hands it can be positively dangerous.

In the case of the newly freed people of the United States in 1776 and 1787, the founders knew and trusted that the citizens understood these things and were prepared for what they had been given. But they also knew what Franklin said that day to Mrs. Powell—that it would take effort, that the great freedoms of the republic they had made possible required keeping. The founders were right in trusting that we would keep the republic and would cultivate the habits of the heart. Based on who we were as a nation at that time it was a good bet, one any wise soul might have taken. But it was impossible for the founders to see where after two centuries the things that were secure in their day would change, that faith could be greatly eroded and then pushed out of the public square via a misunderstanding of the concept of the separation of church and state; and that via many things, such as Vietnam and Watergate, trust in the institutions of government could be damaged—and yet how, ironically and predictably, the people would increasingly assume the government itself could and would do what was necessary.

But we can see it. And we can see that these things have worked against the freedoms the patriots in Washington's Continental Army fought for in overthrowing British tyranny. What, then, is now to be done? What then, are *we* to do?

TWO

The Golden Triangle of Freedom

Liberty cannot be established without morality, nor without faith.

—Alexis de Tocqueville

When I first heard my friend Os Guinness talk about the Golden Triangle of Freedom, I was taken aback.[1] In fact, I was deeply embarrassed, because what he was describing was so central to the idea of American freedom and the American experiment that it seemed inconceivable that somehow I hadn't heard it all before. I was shocked that although I'd attended decent American schools and a top American university, the concept somehow had eluded me entirely. It was not like so many other things one half hears and never retains. It was not like nearly all the math I had learned in high school, or the grammatical concept of the preterite, or Avogadro's number, things on which I conceivably might be refreshed. It was something I had never heard a whisper about in the first place. But as I spoke with people about Os Guinness's book and this concept, I realized I wasn't the only one who had missed it completely. As far as I could tell, no one knew of it. Virtually no one seemed to understand what the founders had taken for granted as the secret center of their novel idea of self-government. This initially seemed impossible to me, but as time passed I had no option but to accept it and then to begin to be terrified about it. If several generations of people had never heard what most previous generations understood, whether explicitly or implicitly, and if this thing really was the secret formula at the center of our fragile and unprecedented form of government, how could America continue much longer? And it led me to my second terrifying question: If America was indeed a country created not because of ethnic or tribal boundaries but instead because a people had come to believe—and therefore embody—a set of ideas, how could America be said to exist if almost no one anymore knew what those ideas were? If these ideas had essentially evaporated from our national consciousness for forty or so years, weren't we unwittingly but unavoidably becoming Americans in name only—if we hadn't already? At what point would that gruesome reality become true, and at what point would that truth be fatal to us? I had in my mind the usually comical image of a cartoon character who, having sped off the edge of a cliff, finds himself standing in midair, thinking quietly, before he suddenly realizes he's no longer on solid ground—and then vanishes speedily out of frame. Were we speeding *toward* the cliff, so that we might still be stopped from speeding beyond it into thin air? Or had we already sped past the edge, with no possibility of return? I'd like to think we still might have a chance of being tackled before we reach the point of no return, but that won't be up to me. It will be up to those of you who are reading this book. No pressure.

I still hope that perhaps those of us who call ourselves Americans might come to understand where we have come from and where we are now, to understand these vital ideas, to remember them again, and to know what it means to be an American. I realize that knowing these things was nothing less than a duty, one of which I had simply been unaware, that it was first and foremost my duty as an American to know what it means to be an American. As I have said, we were charged—in part by Franklin in his famous words—to keep the republic by knowing our duty as Americans and by doing that duty. So first we must understand what it means to be an American, to understand the ideas that we have generally agreed upon together; and then we must know what all of that further entails, lest "we the people" cease to exist, and America cease to exist, and the world be infinitely poorer for it.

I explained part of this in the previous chapter, but now let's look at this idea at the heart of the founders' history-changing vision, what Os Guinness in his writings has resurrected for our generation and what he has named the Golden Triangle of Freedom.

As he succinctly explains in his book *A Free People's Suicide*, the Golden Triangle of Freedom is, when reduced to its most basic form, that freedom requires virtue; virtue requires faith; and faith requires freedom. The three go round and round, supporting one another ad infinitum. If any one of the three legs of the triangle is removed, the whole structure ceases to exist. Let's look now at each of these three legs in turn.

FREEDOM REQUIRES VIRTUE

In the spring of 1787, before the Constitutional Convention of that summer, Benjamin Franklin wrote a short two-paragraph letter to two friends in France, the Abbes Chalut and Arnaud. It had been four years since the end of the revolution, but already the problems with the government they had set up were beginning to show themselves. The Articles of Confederation, which governed the thirteen former colonies, were simply too limited to be effective for a sovereign nation. The most notable example of its shortcomings was shown in the violent uprising that came to be known as Shays' Rebellion. Approximately four thousand Massachusetts citizens actually took up arms against the new national American government. It was eventually put down, but this and other troubles made it clear that something must be done. The founders gathered in Philadelphia to create a government that was stronger than what the Articles of Confederation made possible—but that was not *too* strong. And what they were doing took the form of that document known to us as the Constitution. It would describe the government of the new nation and it would be its legal foundation.

Franklin alludes to the problems they had been having before that summer in the second paragraph of the letter, but it is in the first paragraph that he says something quite surprising to modern American sensibilities. "Only a virtuous people," he declares, "are capable of freedom." It is a staggering statement, especially from Franklin, who was no blue-nosed moralist, nor even a traditional, orthodox Christian. What does he mean by this, and how can he say it so matter-of-factly and so confidently? He is not merely saying that virtue and freedom are linked. He goes far beyond that to say that without one, the other is impossible. If the point isn't clear enough, he goes on to say more. "As nations become corrupt and vicious," he says, "they have more need of masters." The root of the word "vicious" is "vice"—the word simply means "full of vice." So Franklin, without feeling the need to explain himself much, is bluntly saying that "freedom requires virtue." And that less virtue inevitably begets less freedom.

In his day one hardly needed to be a churchgoer to see this.

Franklin had from his earliest days been a proponent of Yankee virtue because it was at the center of the culture in which he had been raised in the Massachusetts Bay Colony. In his *Poor Richard's Almanac,* with its pithy moralistic aphorisms (such as "Early to Bed and Early to Rise Makes a Man Healthy, and Wealthy, and Wise"), and in his *Autobiography* we see countless examples of how Franklin understood the inherent value of virtue in society, apart from what it was that made one virtuous, whether religion or simple cultural habit, or a combination of the two.

Franklin is hardly the only one of the founders who thought this way. Despite their many bitter disagreements on many subjects, the founders were in fact of one mind on this one issue. They all not only agreed on it, but they agreed on it so much as mostly to take it for granted, since it was something that everyone seemed to know. This is, of course, what is so strange to us today. How is it that this thing agreed upon by all the founders as necessary to the form of government they created—and the government we enjoy today—is hardly ever mentioned in our time and is so little known as to be thought forgotten? How can we be Americans if we have mislaid this thing so central to the set of ideas bequeathed to us by the founders?

In June 1776 another of the founders, John Adams—who in contrast to Franklin was a committed and theologically orthodox Christian—made the same point. In a letter to his cousin Zabdiel Adams, he writes: "The only foundation of a free Constitution is pure virtue." Again we must ask ourselves: What world did Adams live in that he could say something like that without the need to explain it or qualify it? And what ideological world do we live in that we are so surprised by it? Adams even went on to warn that if the people of the newly formed United States did not have virtue in "greater measure" in the years ahead than they did when he was writing, they would not have a liberty that would last. "They may change their rulers and the forms of government, but they will not obtain a lasting liberty. They will only exchange tyrants and tyrannies." Adams knew that this was the secret, the thing that would tie it all together.

In the *Federalist Papers*, which serve as a kind of Midrash commentary on the Torah of our founding documents, James Madison too makes the link between virtue and freedom.

> *As there is a degree of depravity in mankind that requires a certain degree of circumspection and distrust, so there are other qualities in human nature that justify a certain portion of esteem and confidence. Republican government presupposes the existence of these qualities in a higher degree than any other form. Were the pictures that have been drawn by the political jealousy of some among us faithful likenesses of the human character, the inference would be, that there is not sufficient virtue among men for self-government; and that nothing less than the*

chains of despotism can restrain them from destroying and devouring one another.

All of the founders understood this. But this idea was not a strange belief limited to the late decades of the eighteenth century. In 1831, some forty years after the Constitution came into being, the French political thinker and historian Alexis de Tocqueville traveled to America with his lifelong friend Gustave de Beaumont. The French government—the so-called July Monarchy—had sent them to examine the prisons and penitentiaries in America, with an eye to bringing what they learned back to France. But his travels and investigations in America would range much farther and wider.

Tocqueville found himself generally marveling at the American people and the democracy they had established that flourished now, over a half century since their revolution. Why had the French Revolution ended in a nightmare of guillotine executions and worse? Why had the French struggled endlessly with political upheavals and violence in the decades since their revolution while America had enjoyed unprecedented success? For America's success to have continued so peacefully for so many decades must have some reason or reasons, and perhaps he could divine them in his time there. When he returned to France, he wrote his now-classic two-volume work, *Democracy in America*. The gist of what Tocqueville concludes may ironically best be summed up in a famous quote misattributed to him since at least 1941.[2] It's such an apt summation of his classic book that no less than Eisenhower, Reagan, and Clinton have used it to illustrate what they too saw as the secret at the heart of American success:

> *Not until I went into the churches of America and heard her pulpits aflame with righteousness did I understand the secret of her genius and power. America is great because she is good, and if America ever ceases to be good, she will cease to be great.*

Though we now know these were someone else's brilliant summation of Tocqueville, we know from the rest of his book that he saw clearly that it was the "goodness" of America's people that made America work. Fifty years after Adams had said it and forty-some years after Franklin had said it, Tocqueville with his own eyes saw the evidence of this wherever he went. For him it was inescapable: *The secret to American freedom was American virtue.* Of course, he didn't mean that Americans were somehow inherently good. No one could or should believe that a disparate group of people on one continent would be somehow inherently better than another group on another continent. That would be akin to racism. This was something about the culture of America, about Americans' shared values. The difference was not in their genetic makeup, nor in their drinking water, nor even in their beliefs. It was in their behavior. That behavior was informed by their beliefs, but if the beliefs hadn't been manifested in their behavior, those beliefs would have made no difference. The word Tocqueville used was "mores"— meaning those habits "of central importance accepted without question and embodying the fundamental moral views of a group." He wrote: "I considered mores to be one of the great general causes responsible for the maintenance of a democratic republic." And then he said that by the term "mores" he meant "habits of the heart." In the same book Tocqueville put it as bluntly as Franklin or Adams had, writing: "Liberty cannot be established without morality."

This idea that freedom of the kind described by the founders requires virtue was central to the thinking of the founding generation and obvious to Tocqueville a half century later. It was the secret at the heart of America.

VIRTUE REQUIRES FAITH

What, then, of the next leg in the Golden Triangle of Freedom? If our modern sensibilities can weather the stormy idea that virtue is inextricably linked to freedom, and that American freedom cannot long be sustained without it, must we also accept the idea that virtue is linked to faith and religion?

Before we consider this idea separately, we should see that for many of the founders the idea of virtue and morality di-

vorced from religion and faith was unthinkable. The link between them was assumed. Perhaps the most famous quotation
on this subject comes to us from John Adams, from a letter he
wrote to the officers in the Massachusetts militia while he was
our second president. That he wrote these words in his official
capacity as U.S. president is itself remarkable to our modern
sensibilities:

> We have no government armed with power capable of
> contending with human passions unbridled by morality
> and religion. Avarice, ambition, revenge, or gallantry,
> would break the strongest cords of our Constitution as a
> whale goes through a net. Our Constitution was made
> only for a moral and religious people. It is wholly inade-
> quate to the government of any other.

Adams understood that the secret to self-government is that
the people must themselves be self-governing, which is to say
they must be motivated by something beyond the law. Each individual must govern himself, and for this morality was plainly
necessary. But in the penultimate sentence Adams conflates
these ideas of morality and religion, because for him—as for
most others of that era—religion was necessary to the success
of the American experiment. It could not and should not be
forced, but it was nonetheless necessary and should certainly be
encouraged, however possible. Adams seems to have had no

idea that future generations might not only miss this, but would loudly argue against it. He seems unable to imagine a world that thinks religion beside the point in this conversation about freedom and self-government, or not just beside the point but somehow antithetical to them. Again, how can we have strayed so far from the founders on these most central points?

But we should ask ourselves: Other than one's religion or faith, what could motivate someone to be virtuous and "self-governing"? Once we understand, as the founders did, that self-government and virtue go hand in hand, we must ask: *What would make someone behave virtuously?* Even if the question is merely pragmatic, we must wonder: Why would someone do the right thing? To be sure, the cultural and societal pressure to conform plays a significant role. But if those things are not enough, what is left to motivate someone in that way? And of course we must ask what motivates that cultural and societal pressure in the first place. For the founders there was little to discuss on this subject. The answer—both practically speaking and theoretically—must be religion. (In our day everyone seems to know that helping the poor is important, for example, or that slavery is wrong, or that being good stewards of the environment is important, but what we have completely forgotten is that these ideas all stemmed from the Judeo-Christian tradition in the West. We seem to think that whatever virtues we do possess arose by themselves. History guffaws at the very idea.)

The founders staked their lives and reputations on these fundamental ideas, but five decades later their bet had been proved safe, because when Tocqueville came to visit, he quickly saw that it was indeed religion that worked hand in hand with American freedom. France had long before fallen far from the high ideals of its revolution, but five decades on, America's freedom shone much as it had in its bright beginning. For Tocqueville religion was clearly the reason.

> *Upon my arrival in the United States the religious aspect of the country was the first thing that struck my attention; and the longer I stayed there, the more I perceived the great political consequences resulting from this new state of things. In France I had almost always seen the spirit of religion and the spirit of freedom marching in opposite directions. But in America I found they were intimately united and that they reigned in common over the same country.*

Tocqueville also said that there was "no country in the world where the Christian religion retains a greater influence over the souls of men than in America." In other words, there is an authority, but it stems from a voluntary—which is to say a free—obedience to God, rather than from forced obedience to any man or government of men.

But he not only observed these things; like the founders, he understood how they worked:

Despotism may govern without faith, but liberty can-
not. Religion is much more necessary in the republic which
they set forth in glowing colors than in the monarchy
which they attack; it is more needed in democratic repub-
lics than in any others. How is it possible that society
should escape destruction if the moral tie is not strength-
ened in proportion as the political tie is relaxed? And
what can be done with a people who are their own mas-
ters if they are not submissive to the Deity?

He understood that the law could not force people to do what was right. In fact, the laws of America didn't try to do this. They provided freedom, and what the citizens did with that freedom was something else altogether. "Thus," Tocqueville writes, "while the law permits the Americans to do what they please, religion prevents them from conceiving, and forbids them to commit, what is rash or unjust."

He also observed that Americans seemed to understand the importance of religion to their way of life and as not less than "indispensable to the maintenance of republican institutions." Tocqueville even goes so far as to say that in the United States, the "sovereign authority is religious." In other words, where there is no human sovereign there must be another sovereign, and for Americans that sovereign was God himself, to whom they would voluntarily submit themselves. Tocqueville writes:

There is no country in the world where the Christian religion retains a greater influence over the souls of men than in America, and there can be no greater proof of its utility and of its conformity to human nature than that its influence is powerfully felt over the most enlightened and free nation of the earth.

George Washington, often wrongly cited as a mere Deist more beholden to the ideas of the French Enlightenment than to Christian faith, concurred on all of the above. In his farewell address at the end of his second term in 1796, he said:

Let us with caution indulge the supposition that morality can be maintained without religion. Whatever may be conceded to the influence of refined education on minds of peculiar structure, reason and experience both forbid us to expect that national morality can prevail in exclusion of religious principles.

According to Washington too the Constitution and the laws of the land were insufficient. Virtue and character were vital; and for these to exist, "religious principles" and "religion" must be present.

But if Franklin and Washington are often mischaracterized as irreligious, none is so mischaracterized as Jefferson himself.

He may well have been the least religious of all the founding fathers, but if he was the least religious, he was nonetheless tremendously religious when compared with the secularism of most of our cultural leaders today. He's wrongly described as the one pure French Enlightenment Deist in the founding scrum, but this can hardly be true, because the principles that motivated the French Revolution were not only secular but also violently anticlerical, and Jefferson nowhere comes close to this characterization. It can only be that the zeal of modern secularists has caused Jefferson's irreligiosity to be exaggerated and that intellectual sloppiness has allowed many of us to accept that blurred view. Who but a man who believed in God and who took God seriously as an agent in history could write what Jefferson wrote in his *Notes on the State of Virginia* in 1785:

> *Can the liberties of a nation be thought secure when we have removed their only firm basis, a conviction in the minds of the people, that those liberties are the gift of God? That they are violated but with his wrath? I tremble for my country when I reflect that God is just, and that His justice cannot sleep for ever.*

If we suppose he is talking about a clockmaker God of Deist imagination and not the Yahweh of the Hebrew Scriptures, we should consider his letter to Daniel Webster in which he says: "I have always said, and always will say, that the studious perusal of the [Bible] will make better citizens, better fathers, and better husbands."[3]

But once we have seen that the founders unanimously thought virtue necessary to freedom and religion necessary to virtue, we must ask: What allowed religion itself to thrive as it did? And now we have come full circle—or full triangle, if you will—because Guinness says that it is freedom itself that makes religion and faith thrive in America.

FAITH REQUIRES FREEDOM

The idea that freedom requires virtue, which requires faith—which in turn requires freedom—is at once simple and elegant, but to our modern and often secularly inclined minds it can be a bit disturbing. For many the idea of faith and freedom working together to bolster each other brings about cognitive dissonance. That's because in America today we have stepped backward to a cultural situation less like the earlier times in our own country than like the France of Tocqueville's day, in which religion and freedom were thought to be bitterest enemies.

"In France," Tocqueville wrote, "I had almost always seen the spirit of religion and the spirit of freedom marching in opposite directions. But in America I found they were intimately united and that they reigned in common over the same country."

America in the twenty-first century has generally returned to the worldview of the eighteenth-century French Enlightenment rationalists, who were so appalled at the religious wars of the previous century that they recoiled from all religion, unable to fathom a world in which religion and freedom could be mutually supporting. England too, had become generally skeptical of the orthodox Christian faith, especially among its cultural elites, and many Church of England pastors were themselves preaching a kind of French Enlightenment rationalism from their state-sanctioned pulpits. But Tocqueville saw the error in such thinking and saw that the truth of the matter was borne out in American society.

> *The philosophers of the eighteenth century explained in a very simple manner the gradual decay of religious faith. Religious zeal, said they, must necessarily fail the more generally liberty is established and knowledge diffused. But the facts by no means accord with their theory. There are certain populations in Europe whose unbelief is only equaled by their ignorance and debasement; while in America, one of the freest and most enlightened nations in the world, the people fulfill with fervor all the outward duties of religion.*

The eighteenth-century philosophes have many indignant children in the West today, but time and again the facts of history stubbornly repel their prognostications. Those who have maintained that religion would evaporate as knowledge and liberties increase see that this is somehow not at all the case. The "God of the gaps" does in fact go away, but the true God of history only reveals himself the more.

But what is it about *American* religion that defies the predictions of the French Enlightenment secularists? What haven't they accounted for? In another place Tocqueville writes:

> *The character of Anglo-American civilization . . . is the product . . . of two perfectly distinct elements that elsewhere have often made war with each other, but which, in America, they have succeeded in incorporating somehow into one another and combining marvelously. I mean to speak of the spirit of religion and the spirit of freedom.*

But how is one a buttress to the other? For sure the main difference between how the founders saw faith and how most other societies saw faith had everything to do with what we in America call religious freedom or religious liberty. This did not exist in France, nor anywhere in Europe during this period. But in America, from the very beginning, it did. It was this that thwarted the predictions of the French Enlightenment philosophes and it is this that continues to thwart the predictions of modern secularists. Of course, Tocqueville saw it himself:

> *The sects that exist in the United States are innumerable. They all differ in respect to the worship which is due*

to the Creator; but they all agree in respect to the duties which are due from man to man. Each sect adores the Deity in its own peculiar manner, but all sects preach the same moral law in the name of God. . . . Moreover, all the sects of the United States are comprised within the great unity of Christianity, and Christian morality is everywhere the same.

Since the Pilgrims came to our shores in 1620, religious freedom and religious tolerance have been the single most important principle of American life. This was the genius at the heart of it all. But tragically this linchpin of American liberty has been more misunderstood in recent years than at any time in our existence. So let's take a moment to dilate on that subject.

WHAT IS RELIGIOUS LIBERTY?

Danbury, Connecticut, the town where I grew up, is often remembered as "Hat City"—or the "hat capital" of the world. By 1800 it made more hats than any other city in America; and in 1887 it boasted thirty hat factories producing five million hats per year. But by the time the hatlessly fashionable President Kennedy was inaugurated in 1960, hats fell precipitously out of fashion, and just a few years later Danbury's last hat factory closed. Nonetheless all of the high school sports teams are still known as the Hatters and the school mascot is a beaver in a bowler. Danbury is also often noted as the birthplace of the composer Charles Ives.

But what Danbury ought to be most famous for is rarely mentioned or acknowledged, even among us natives of that fair city. We are now talking about a letter written on the first day of 1802 to the Danbury Baptist Association by then-President Thomas Jefferson. In it Jefferson coins the phrase "wall of separation between church and state," but the phrase has since become so well known that today many believe it to be in the Constitution itself. It exists only in that letter to the Baptist Association of my hometown, but it's become a shorthand way of talking about the Establishment Clause in the Constitution, expressing the idea that the national government cannot take sides with one church over another. This is an astonishing notion in the history of the world, that a state would not be directly or officially affiliated with a religious institution.

But what Jefferson said in that letter and what the founders said in the Constitution was not something new in America. Almost from the beginning, America had operated in a way different from the rest of the world where this issue was concerned.

We know that the Pilgrims fled England and then Holland because they were being persecuted for their faith, and they sought to worship freely in the new country to which they traveled. But this idea of religious freedom would go much further in a few decades. In 1657 in Queens, New York—where I was born—in the town of Flushing (then called Vlishing), something called the Flushing Remonstrance was written, in which thirty residents of the small Dutch settlement petitioned Peter Stuyvesant against his prohibition of Quaker worship. That document is widely considered a precursor to our own constitutional ideas on religious liberty. And in 1663 the charter of Roger Williams's Colony of Rhode Island said:

> No person within the said colony, at any time hereafter, shall be in any wise molested, punished, disquieted or called in question, for any differences in opinion in matters of religion, and who do not actually disturb the civil peace of our said colony; but that all . . . may from time to time, and at all times hereafter, freely and fully have and enjoy his and their own judgments and consciences, in matters of religious concernments.

So 124 years before the Constitution and 139 years before Jefferson's famous letter to the Danbury Baptists, an American document was establishing this idea of religious liberty as sacrosanct, so to speak, as a central component of American freedom. There are two principal reasons that this happened in the American colonies. The first was what the historian Paul Johnson has called the "Erasmian nature of religious America, which was and is concerned with moral conduct rather than dogma."

One sees this plainly almost everywhere one looks in colonial America. Johnson tells us:

> *American religious groups were judged not by their theology but by the behavior of their adherents. Thus the very diversity of the sects constituted the national religious strength, since all operated within a broad common code of morals, and their competition for souls mirrored the competition of firms for business in the market economy. In both cases the role of the state was to hold the ring and make that competition fair.*

That is what religious liberty was and is. The government essentially said, *Yes, be religious. We will not only tolerate it; we will respect it and we will encourage it. But we cannot take sides or put our thumbs on the scales.* But the understanding of this has been lost to many in modern America.

Today we well understand this impartiality when it comes to the competition of corporations. We need only to imagine the disappearance of that impartiality to see it all the clearer. Imagine if one day the United States government decided that it would favor Apple but would look askance at Microsoft. Imagine that it used taxpayer money to buy Apple products for all employees of the federal government. And imagine that it also helped prop up Apple in other ways. Most Americans would instinctively know that wasn't fair, that the government simply cannot and must not do that sort of thing. If it did, we would effectively cease to be America. That's the sort of behavior one expects in corrupt nations or in communist nations, but not here.

In the financial meltdown of 2008 we saw something like this begin to happen. The government said that for the sake of the nation, it would have to prop up some corporations because they were "too big to fail"—meaning that if they went under the whole country would suffer. So the federal government decided it would step in and use your taxpayer money to bail out certain select companies—but not bail out other companies. In other words, the government began deciding who could fail and who must win. It was a scary moment for America, this idea that the government, with all its power and resources, could begin to take sides in that way.

We've always believed that for America to thrive, the free market must be left alone. We might have some regulations and some antitrust laws, but generally that would be to make the playing field more even, not less. But how does that principle of freedom work when we're talking not about economic freedom but about religious freedom?

This brings us back to the Constitution. The founders wrote that the government could not "establish" a religion. This meant that the government could never favor one religion over another. One of the main reasons the United States came into being was because people had left Europe, where this "establishment" of religion was going on all the time and was manifestly monstrous and destructive to individual freedom. People's lives were ruined if they didn't choose the "right" religion. The founders knew that the country they were hoping to live in must be nothing like that. Everyone must be free to decide what religion he would choose—and the government would not choose any religion. It would be impartial toward all of them.

Indeed, because America was the place to which so many who were being persecuted for their religious beliefs in Europe repaired, it became a place where many Christian denominations lived cheek by jowl. The main thing was not that one belong to the right church but that all churches live in a way that upheld the common good. Simply put, the differences among the denominations were practically less important than their similarities.

In his *Autobiography* Franklin relates how in 1739, when George Whitefield had come to Philadelphia, finding all of the churches closed to him (for reasons we will learn in our next chapter), Franklin proposed a place of meeting where Whitefield— and anyone else—could speak about God and religion. Whitefield had no difficulty preaching outside, as we will soon see, but Franklin thought that there ought to be a place where Whitefield and others could promote faith and the ideas of faith. He saw it as vital to the thriving of society.

And it being found inconvenient to assemble in the open Air, subject to its Inclemencies, the Building of a

*House to meet in was no sooner propos'd and Persons ap-
pointed to receive Contributions.... Both House and
Ground were vested in Trustees, expressly for the Use of
any Preacher of any religious Persuasion who might desire
to say something to the People of Philadelphia, the Design
[purpose] in building not being to accommodate any particular Sect, but the Inhabitants in general, so that even if
the Mufti of Constantinople were to send a Missionary to
preach Mahometanism [Islam] to us, he would find a Pulpit at his Service.*

This was the genius of the founders, to separate church and
state in such a way that they were each sacrosanct.

To sum up, the one thing that was necessary for self-
government—and the United States—to exist and function was
religion, but religion itself could not properly function unless
religion were detached from the government. Only when religion was truly free could it be *true* religion—and only then
could all other freedoms follow. That this was never possible
until the last years of the eighteenth century tells us that it is not
a naturally occurring phenomenon. Many things had to be in
place for it to be possible. But there were two crucial things that
must be put in place for all of it to work, and these two things
were not planned by anyone, nor could they have been. One was
that the colonies would somehow be more united than they
were at the beginning of that century, and the other was that the

citizens of those colonies possessed a much deeper understanding of self-government and of the faith that would make it possible. Happily these two things came into existence nonetheless. But how? We might simply say that providence brought them into existence. We might also say that providence brought them into existence through the life and work of a single man, very little known to us today. We are talking about the life and work of the man named George Whitefield, without whom the United States simply could not have come into being. His extraordinary story is one of the most astonishing ellipses in our history, and perhaps in history generally.

THREE

"The Wonder of the Age"

In early November 1739 a slight, cross-eyed twenty-four-year-old Englishman stepped off a ship in the bustling harbor of Philadelphia. His arrival there was anticipated by nearly everyone who had followed his historic exploits across the ocean throughout that summer in the *Pennsylvania Gazette*, published by thirty-three-year-old Benjamin Franklin. No fewer than four thousand were jostling to catch a glimpse of him. By the time Whitefield walked down the gangplank onto the Philadelphia dock, he was already an impossibly famous celebrity. Not until two centuries later, when the Beatles landed at

New York's Idlewild Airport, would a British export to America create such giddiness. But why?

The boyish figure in question was a preacher, but he was a preacher unlike any the Philadelphia crowd had heard of before. He was a phenomenon whose voice was of such singular quality that all across England many people who heard it were quite undone, weeping and crying out to God. Even such worldly sophisticates as the actor David Garrick and the philosopher David Hume had gone to hear this man, who was routinely drawing crowds numbering twenty to thirty thousand.

At the very beginning of his ministry, Whitefield had been warmly welcomed into churches. But in time most respectable ministers found his message and methods shocking and objectionable, so they pointedly shut their doors to him. But this would backfire magnificently when Whitefield took to preaching out of doors. The effects of this were not less than electric. Before anyone knew it, many thousands were swarming to hear him and the Church of England establishment could do little besides sputter with indignant rage. How outrageous it was that their flocks should be siphoned away by this queer, otherworldly fellow! But then he would travel to the colonies—and good riddance!

In fact, Whitefield had been to America just over a year earlier, at the invitation of his friends John and Charles Wesley, whom he had known at Oxford. He had preached extensively and tirelessly in the few months he was there, as he always did and would for the subsequent entirety of his life, but all of that was small beer compared with what lay ahead now.

Just as in England, Whitefield first preached in churches, and just as in England, once the ministers decided they had had enough of him, he took to open-air preaching. Again the numbers that would now come to hear him were historic. Ever the Yankee skeptic, Benjamin Franklin wondered how someone so physically insubstantial could be heard by twenty or thirty thousand. So one evening, when Whitefield was preaching from the top of the courthouse steps, the canny amateur scientist undertook an experiment. Years later he wrote of it in his *Autobiography*:

> *[Whitefield] had a loud and clear voice, and articulated his words in sentence so perfectly that he might be heard and understood at a great distance, especially as his auditories, however numerous, observed the most exact silence. He preached one evening from the top of the Court-house steps, which are in the middle of Market Street, and on the west side of Second Street, which crosses it at right angles. Both streets were filled with his hearers to a considerable distance. Being among the hindmost in Market Street, I had the curiosity to learn how far he could be heard, by retiring backwards down the street towards the river; and I found his voice distinct till I came near Front Street, when some noise in that street obscured*

it. Imagining then a semicircle, of which my distance should be the radius, and that it were filled with auditors, to each of whom I allow two square feet, I computed that he might well be heard by more than thirty thousand. This reconciled me to the newspaper accounts of his having preached to twenty-five thousand people in the fields, and to the ancient histories of generals haranguing whole armies, of which I had sometimes doubted.

When Franklin conducted this experiment in November 1739, Pennsylvania was one of thirteen British colonies, none of which had any idea that thirty years in the future they might be thinking of independence. Their people were naturally deferential to authority but already markedly less than their counterparts in Britain across the sea. The American character was emerging and Franklin more than anyone embodied it. He was the proverbial self-made man who had left kith and kin in Boston to start life anew in Philadelphia at age seventeen and had by his own wits and ingenuity achieved tremendous things, and would achieve many more in the years ahead. But still, the idea of self-rule, of self-government—of throwing off the yoke of the British Empire and forging ahead alone—was at that time still quite far off, a cloud the size of a man's fist on the horizon. But it was the man preaching at the top of the courthouse steps who more than anyone would change that. It would take three decades of his tireless preaching, but by the time he died in 1770, the colonies would be united in a way that was unthinkable when he arrived, and their people would have so changed their attitudes toward authority and toward monarchy that they would have become a different kind of people than had ever before existed in the world. The small cloud on the horizon would have become a torrential downpour.

To truly understand the story of how the United States of America came into existence, we must acquaint ourselves with the human weather pattern known as the Reverend George Whitefield.

COMING TO AMERICA

George Whitefield was born into humble circumstances in the Bell Inn in Gloucester, the youngest of seven children. His parents owned and ran the inn, which still stands today. From the earliest age he was seen to possess tremendous talent as an actor. His voice was remarkably melodious, so much so that decades later the world-famous actor David Garrick would declare, "I would give a hundred guineas, if I could say 'Oh' like Mr. Whitefield." In fact, his vocal talents were so astonishing that they would end up playing a vital role in the creation of the modern world.

The quirky story of how this came to pass began when Whitefield was fifteen. His father had died when he was two, and when he came to his teens he saw that he could never afford to go to university, though he clearly had the mind and inclination to do so. Being a realist, however, he immediately abandoned his schooling and gave himself over to helping his mother run the inn. She needed the help badly and accepted his offer. So young Whitefield donned a blue apron and spent his time washing mops, cleaning rooms, and doing whatever else was necessary to properly run a public inn.

Then one day a visitor to the inn put forward a startling idea: Perhaps Whitefield could go up to Oxford after all. He could do it, the man explained, if he was willing to be what was called a "servitor." This was the term given to those young men who served the other students, polishing their shoes and generally being butler and maid. It was looked upon as humiliating work, but Whitefield had been doing these things at the Bell Inn for years. He was not only used to it but also very good at it. So with little hesitation and much enthusiasm, he now reversed course. He would return to his schooling and prepare for Oxford.

But over the last few years something else had been happening in Whitefield's life. His father's death and the subsequent difficulties of his mother's second marriage had driven Whitefield to think about God. On his own the precocious young fellow had begun reading certain books, the chief of which was the Bible, and he had found that the ideas they contained gave him great comfort. So by the time he entered Oxford's Pembroke College, Whitefield was of a decidedly pious bent, especially when compared with the other students, who seemed in a perpetual contest to best one another in roguish behavior. When one day some of his chamber mates tried to pull him into their bad habits, George made it clear he wasn't interested, preferring to be quite alone most of the time, if that's what was necessary. It was. And so he would be a loner for some time.

But also at Oxford during this period—in Lincoln College, where their rooms are preserved to this day—were a certain Charles and John Wesley. They were also of a pious bent and had formed a group called the Holy Club, which gathered to pray and study the Bible regularly. In the riotous atmosphere of the time, the members of this club were, of course, generally reviled and mocked, but whenever George heard them disparaged he vigorously rose to their defense. In fact, he longed to join them in their Holy Club; but being a servitor, he was not allowed to speak with the Wesleys directly. Circumstances, however, finally led the Wesleys to notice George, and one day Charles approached him and invited him into their society. What happened next in that Holy Club is one of those things we may properly think of as a hinge in the history of the world—a point on which everything turns.

There were then about fifteen members in the Holy Club. They prayed together several times per week and also studied the Scriptures regularly. And since the Scriptures did not concern themselves only with one's intellectual and prayer life, but with how one treated others, especially those who were poor and suffering, this group also did many good works, including visiting prisoners and those who were ill and teaching orphans how to read. They also fasted every Wednesday and Friday and took communion once a week at St. Mary's Church. This group was so methodical in how they spent their time that the other Oxford students eventually dubbed them "methodists," though in time they would take the term as a badge of honor and the historical movement that eventually bore their name became known as the "Methodist movement."

It would seem the behavior of these young men couldn't be improved upon, but when Whitefield read a book titled *The Life of God in the Soul of Man,* by a seventeenth-century divine named Henry Scougal, he got other ideas. One passage in particular struck him:

> Some place [the Christian faith] in ... orthodox notions and opinions. Others place it in the outward man, in a constant course of external duties and a model of performances; if they live peaceably with their neighbours, keep a temperate diet, observe the returns of worship, frequenting the church or their closet, and sometimes extend their hands to the relief of the poor, they think they have sufficiently acquitted himself.

But Scougal said that all of these things are not what makes one a Christian. If anyone might have had his interest piqued by this, it would be George Whitefield. He had done all these things with tremendous zeal, but Scougal made it clear that these were all beside the main point of the Christian faith. "True Religion is an Union of the Soul with God," Scougal said. It is "a real participation of the divine nature, the very image of God drawn upon the Soul, or in the Apostle's phrase, it is Christ formed within us." These words struck George with tremendous force. He saw that he was somehow missing the very heart of the faith, but what he did in response is almost comical in its wrongheadedness. He immediately vigorously redoubled his efforts, embracing a program of self-denial that nearly killed him.

To begin with, he refused to eat any foods that he liked, especially fruit. He also thought being concerned with his appearance was nothing but vanity, so he stopped powdering his hair, as was the custom then. When his college gown ripped, he decided he must not have it mended, because that too would be a sign of vanity, and he refused to clean his shoes. It seemed that George Whitefield was determined to glorify God by becoming a slovenly, tattered wreck. As a result of all this, he lost some of his work as a servitor, as not everyone employing him fancied being served by a dirty, otherworldly vagabond.

But George was not through denying himself yet. Before the madness of his religious fanaticism could bear full fruit, he would give up laughter too. He believed that he must find joy only in praying and worshipping God, so suddenly jokes and mirth were strictly *verboten*. Then one day Whitefield recalled that Jesus had spent all night praying on a mountainside alone, so after praying in his room he took his prayers outside into the damp of the early English winter, walking across the street to Christ Church Walk and kneeling down on the damp turf to pray. After thirty minutes he realized kneeling wasn't the limit of how he could abase himself before God, and he lay flat on the cold ground. Then it began to rain. Whatever breakthrough he had been seeking eluded him, however, and he finally got up and returned to his room, nonetheless resolving to do this again and again in the weeks to come.

Meanwhile there were still other joys that must be killed. George even decided to forgo the pleasure of his friends' company, so instead of praying with the Holy Club he elected to pray only by himself. By now John and Charles had begun to worry about their overzealous little friend. John paid George a visit and convinced him that he might be taking things a bit too far. Could it be that praying with his friends was not something that God wanted him to give up? George eventually conceded the point and promised to join their meetings again—but his other austere activities would continue all the same. For example, by way of food he now subsisted almost solely on coarse bread and sage tea without sugar.

But at last something would stop him in this forbidding course. He was one day walking near Magdalen Bridge when a bedraggled woman staggered toward him. She was the wife of one of the prisoners he had been visiting. She was soaked to the skin and blurted to George that she had just tried to drown herself right there in the Cherwell River. She said that she had done this because her children were starving and she couldn't bear it anymore. But she explained that a gentleman had seen her in the water and had rescued her. She then realized the terrible sin of what she was doing and wished to repent. In fact, she had that very minute been looking for Mr. Whitefield! She knew he would show her the way to true salvation. So George immediately gave her some money and made an appointment to meet her and her husband at the jail later that day.

When he arrived at the prison, George decided to read to the couple from the third chapter of the Gospel of John. He spoke the famous verse from John 3:16—"For God so loved the world that he gave his only begotten son, that whoever believes in him should not perish but have everlasting life"—and upon hearing these simple words, the woman nearly sprang heavenward. She was deeply affected. Suddenly she declared "I believe!" over and over. "I am born again!" she shouted. "I am saved!" Soon her husband understood it as well and joined these ejaculations. The two of them were changed before George's goggling eyes. As far as they were concerned, the message was simple and clear. All they must do is believe! But it was a flustering experience for George. He wasn't ready to take these words at their simple face value just yet. So for weeks after this episode he continued his life of draconian self-denial.

After six months of this dire behavior, he predictably grew

quite ill. Day after day he lay in bed, praying and barely eating. During this time he picked up another old book, *Contemplations on the New Testament* by a certain Joseph Hall. George found its tone reassuring and calming, but when he came to a passage about the thief dying on the cross beside Jesus, it was as though scales fell from his eyes, just as they had from the eyes of the woman and her husband in the prison. George realized that the thief hadn't done anything except believe, and no sooner had the thief declared this than Jesus said, "Today you will be with me in paradise."

What followed from this moment in a bed in Oxford's Pembroke College can hardly be calculated. It was as if in the dead works doldrums the slightest finger of a divine breeze blew that day, which over the course of the next weeks and months and years would become a sanctified tornado. It would reconfigure things in England and then leap across the Atlantic to light down in the New World and there so dramatically alter the landscape of the thirteen colonies that we really should not think of anything that has happened since without first thinking of that tornado.

But first George must recuperate. So immediately after this epiphany George returned home to the Bell Inn. But even while regaining his health, he ministered to the poor and sick and to prisoners, telling them of his new discovery. The bishop of Gloucester took notice of the zealous twenty-one-year-old. The youngest age at which someone could then be ordained was twenty-three, but the bishop now very happily made an exception.

George's first sermon after his ordination was at St. Mary de Crypt, where he had himself been baptized and taken his first communion. A very large crowd appeared to see this preternaturally youthful native son in the pulpit. He was so young that some in attendance openly mocked him, but eventually the gale force of his talent and message silenced the crowd, who became enraptured. All in attendance agreed they had never heard his equal. In fact, someone afterward complained to the bishop that no less than fifteen persons had been driven quite mad. Thus commenced a preaching career without equal in the two-thousand-year history of the Christian church.

Word of mouth traveled quickly and invitations from London soon followed. The young man's exploding reputation pulled people from such highways and byways as no one knew had existed. Already in the first months of his preaching he had become a phenomenon, infuriating many ministers, who didn't like the idea of this upstart waking their sleepy flocks. On the positive side it was said that Whitefield's voice "startled England like a trumpet blast."

By this time George's old friends the Wesleys had crossed the great Atlantic to Georgia to minister as missionaries to the Indians there. Seeing the great spiritual hunger in that part of the world, they soon invited George to join them, and he cheerfully accepted. But when it became known he would be leaving

England—perhaps for good—many tried to stop him, and the numbers who came to hear him increased the more. In these first months of his preaching career, George Whitefield preached many times every day. He preached wherever they would have him, and in some places that they wouldn't. He preached in prisons and he preached to soldiers and every Sunday he preached in not one but several churches. Impossibly, this breakneck, whirlwind pace would continue unabated for the next thirty-three years, until he had by the time of his death preached the unheard-of number of eighteen thousand sermons, along with twelve thousand "talks and exhortations." No one before or since has ever approached such figures.

Even on the ship to Savannah Whitefield preached often, and when they arrived in Georgia he continued just as he had in England, preaching twice per day and four times on Sundays. After a few months he traveled to South Carolina and preached there, but at long last he felt he must return to London and on September 6, 1738, began the journey from Charleston harbor. But now when he returned to England, he first saw strong opposition to what he was saying and how he was saying it.

There were various aspects to the phenomenon of George Whitefield that made him so popular with most who heard him and so unpopular with some others. He was saying things people had never heard in their lives, and he was saying those things in a way they had never heard before. Some people went half mad with enthusiasm, crying out and carrying on in a way that was decidedly frowned upon in the upper classes. After all, gentlemen and ladies mustn't be exposed to such vulgar and buffoonish displays of emotion. But there was no stopping what was happening, and it's not too much to say that the cultural earthquake begat by Elvis and the Beatles in recent times is as close as we can come to understanding what Whitefield represented. His preaching signaled the first rays of the dawning of a new order in the world. But would that new order be something good or bad? But what would it look like if these forces remained unchecked? No one knew.

So the unscripted freedom and wildness of the vast crowds disturbed and threatened those who had a stake in the status quo. Many ministers accused Whitefield of "enthusiasm"—a derisive term for anything that departed from the starched, constricting order of their traditional Anglican services. Of course, for someone who had been dully laboring in a pulpit for decades to see this histrionic young fellow draw thousands must have been irksome. So one after another of the pulpits that had been open to him were shut for fear that he was spreading a dangerous doctrine.

But more than anything that would distinguish the faith of Whitefield and that would loft him into the empyrean realm of history changers was the simple fact that he was not too proud to go to people wherever they might be found. If the established churches would not receive him, he would like his master go out into the highways and byways; he would preach in prisons and anywhere else he might be received. But one day he did something else along these lines, something that no one had seen in their lifetimes.

The idea first alit upon Mr. Whitefield's crown one Sunday when he was preaching at the Bermondsey Church in South London. So many had turned out to see him that day that even after the church was crammed to capacity, about a thousand remained outside in the churchyard among the tombstones and crypts, straining to hear him through the open windows. As he preached from the pulpit, he had the idea of perhaps going outside and standing on top of one of the larger tombstones and preaching from there. He didn't do it that day, but he later mentioned the idea to some friends, who thought it a "mad notion," although they knelt and prayed about it with him nonetheless.

Two weeks later this germ bore fruit when he traveled to Bristol, to an area inhabited primarily by uneducated and unchurched persons of the wildest sort, most of whom labored in the coal mines there. These colliers had no church to go to and Whitefield's heart went out to them. "I thought," he said, "it might be doing the service of my Creator, who had a mountain for his pulpit, and the heavens for a sounding board." So on the late afternoon of February 17, 1739—a Tuesday—he climbed to the top of a mound in a place called Rose Green in Kingston and began to preach. He had done nothing to advertise his presence that day, but about two hundred who were walking home from the mines gathered around to see and hear him, who must have appeared the strangest curiosity. Most of them had never been to a church in their lives, and the sight of this young man preaching drew their attention. What was he saying?

The next day that he preached there, the crowd numbered in the thousands—and the third time he did so there was a throng of nearly twenty thousand, many of them with faces still blackened by the coal dust that was the hazard of their occupation. No respectable minister in the Church of England would travel to such a godforsaken precinct, much less preach to these befouled savages, but Whitefield was doing what he knew Jesus had done: He was taking medicine to those who knew they were sick and offering freedom to those who knew they were captives. His heart went out to these despised outcasts, and with everything he had in him he preached to these men and women under the evening sky. He later wrote that the "first discovery of their being affected was to see the white gutters made by their tears, which plentifully fell down their black cheeks, as they came out of their coal pits." Many thousands of these men and women received his message of salvation and freedom that day with great emotion.

All of this was taking place in an era when such things were unheard of. To many churchgoers the idea of preaching out of doors was an affront to decency, like attending a funeral without a shirt. But to those who never went to church, it was a tremendous opportunity, one they didn't take for granted.

In our time there are innumerable spectacles held out of doors, from concerts to fireworks displays. And the poorest in our nation suffer not from a lack of entertainment and spectacle but from a surfeit. But in the time of Whitefield the only outdoor events to which the uncouth masses could flock were grotesque displays of animal cruelty, such as bullbaitings and bearbaitings—or public hangings. On some occasions the executed criminal would even be publicly dissected. These events were invariably filled with drunkenness and rowdiness.

But for these humble wretches to be able to hear something good and beautiful—and actually aimed at them—was a dream, one they hadn't expected any more than they would have expected to eat strawberries and cream from a silver spoon. The notion that anyone cared about them seems not to have existed. That the poor and uneducated have value is something we today take for granted, but it is something that came into history only because of what began here, when this young man announced to the unwashed rabble that there was someone who cared about them, who loved them, and who sought their company. To a man or woman born into that brutal world, it must have been a revelation, as though heaven itself had opened and they could hear their names pronounced by the tongues of angels.

As there are today, so there were then several modes of resistance to his message. Some Church of England pulpits preached a withering, pinched sort of castor-oil moralism, while others preached a comforting and soapy lukewarm Deism, which was essentially nothing more than French Enlightenment rationalism. But Whitefield knew that these counterfeits had left many longing for the truth and the freedom of the Gospel, and he would let nothing stop him from reaching these hungry souls, wherever they might be found.

Much of what made him so compelling was that his audiences could see that he himself was affected by the power of what he spoke. The God of whom he spoke and the love of God were so real to Whitefield that others were drawn into the powerful current of his own emotions. Whitefield's assistant in later years, Cornelius Winter, said, "I hardly ever knew him to go through a sermon without weeping. . . . Sometimes he exceedingly wept, stamped loudly and passionately, and was frequently so overcome, that, for a few seconds, you would suspect he never could recover."

And so during this time in England he became the phenomenon of that time. But what was he saying that some felt such a threat to the social order? For one thing, Whitefield preached that everyone was equal in the sight of God, that the beggar and the duchess alike were sinners in need of a savior. But to elevate the lower classes to any kind of equality with their social superiors seemed to many the zenith of recklessness and folly. To those in the lower and middle classes, however, it was truth and beauty. They'd never heard anything like it, and certainly not from a pulpit.

Many felt the Church of England was little more than an

extension of the Crown, a glowering authority with a vested interest in keeping everyone out of mischief, and with a captive audience that couldn't choose to go elsewhere. To those with ecclesiastical power, Whitefield's egalitarian and emotional messages must have seemed as though Dionysus himself had arrived and was cavorting with his maenads through their congregations. It was all a great scandal that must be stopped as soon as possible. Like Euripides' Pentheus, the mandarins of social order could only seethe at these offenses against decorum.

But it was precisely this contrast that shows us Whitefield's subsequent appeal to the American colonists in the years and decades ahead. Just as jazz and Elvis would represent a threat to the order of their time, they also represented the very life and joy and freedom and wildness inherent in the promise of America. It was a two-edged sword, to be sure, and could always go too far. In France, for example, similar things would lead to the chaos and bloodbath of the French Revolution, and in the United States the sexual revolution of the sixties would lead not only to greater personal freedom but also to the social chaos brought on by the breakdown of the family.

Whitefield's principal message concerned what he called the "new birth." After his own experience in Oxford, he knew that the Christian faith was not about how one behaved but about what one believed, and if one truly believed one could do nothing to achieve salvation but believe in Jesus, one's behavior would follow. So everywhere he went he preached what was for that time a revolutionary message. Since the 1970s in America there has been much talk of being "born again," and no less than President Jimmy Carter famously declared himself to have been a "born-again" Christian. But in Whitefield's day it was a new and particularly grating notion, especially to those in power, who felt that they were naturally superior to those in the laboring classes. That everyone might be "born again" and therefore in an instant rendered somehow equal did not digest well. Furthermore, the notion that those in power should themselves require this "new birth" to be justified in the eyes of God was an affront. Like the Pharisees of Jesus's day, they thought they were already perfectly fine and were deeply offended that this young fellow should be telling them that their years of attending church services hadn't turned the magical key that let them into God's kingdom. So when Whitefield returned to England now, the establishment churches had had enough time to figure all of this out, and they shut their doors to him as quickly as they had opened them two years before.

Whitefield knew what he was up against. He understood that many, if not most, of the ministers in the Church of England were themselves merely going through their religious motions in jobs that were little more than sinecures. Many of them were therefore complete strangers to this startling message of God's grace and redemption for all. But when they became openly hostile to Whitefield and his message, he began to point out their spiritual shortcomings publicly in his writings, infuriating them the more.

But all of this was as it were preparation for what would happen when Whitefield again crossed the ocean for the colonies. During his lifetime he would cross the Atlantic thirteen times, but it was this second trip to America that would forever alter the landscape of the New World, which in turn would affect the rest of the world. Because it would unite that scattering of peoples into a single people, one that together saw the world differently than any had before and that was prepared to depart from history in a way none had ever done. What would happen during his time in the thirteen colonies would begin the process of uniting them into something greater than the sum of their disparate parts, would begin the process of preparing them to become the United States of America.

BORN AGAIN

Whitefield left for his second journey to America on August 14, 1739. As we have already seen, his arrival in Philadelphia was greeted with tremendous enthusiasm. The first morning he preached to six thousand and that afternoon to eight thousand. On Sunday fifteen thousand came to hear him. Benjamin Franklin, though never officially a Christian, was nonetheless immediately impressed by Whitefield. "Every accent," Franklin said, "every emphasis, every modulation of voice, was so perfectly turned, and well-placed, that without being interested in the subject, one could not help being pleased with the discourse." He said it was much like listening to "an excellent piece of music."

Whitefield was perpetually raising funds for an orphanage the Wesleys wished to build in Georgia. The legendarily thrifty Franklin was firmly convinced that Whitefield never spent a penny on himself, but one day he counseled Whitefield that it would be far more prudent to save the money required in transporting the building materials to Georgia by building his orphanage right there in Philadelphia—and bringing the Georgian orphans to the orphanage. Whitefield rejected this idea and, while he wished his friend well, Franklin vowed that he wouldn't give any more money to the endeavor, no matter how noble it was. But Whitefield's abilities to persuade were considerable, as Franklin tells us:

> *I happened soon after to attend one of his sermons, in the course of which I perceived he intended to finish with a collection, and I silently resolved he should get nothing from me. I had in my pocket a handful of copper money, three or four silver dollars, and five pistoles in gold. As he proceeded I began to soften, and concluded to give the coppers. Another stroke of his oratory made me ashamed of that, and determined me to give the silver; and he finished so admirably, that I emptied my pocket wholly into the collector's dish, gold and all. At this sermon there was*

also one of our club, who, being of my sentiments respecting the building and Georgia, and suspecting a collection might be intended, had, by precaution, emptied his pockets before he came from home. Towards the conclusion of the discourses, however, he felt a strong desire to give, and applied to a neighbor, who stood near him, to borrow some money for the purpose. The application was unfortunately [made] to perhaps the only man in the company who had the firmness not to be affected by the preacher. His answer was, "At any other time, Friend Hopkinson, I would lend to thee freely; but not now, for thee seems to be out of thy right sense."

Although Franklin never quite accepted the whole of Whitefield's theology, the effect of Whitefield's preaching met with his approval. From his earliest years he had been a believer in virtuous behavior, and he saw that the hundreds who were being converted by Whitefield's preaching became model citizens, so he did all he could to promote Whitefield, publishing his entire sermons on the front page of the *Pennsylvania Gazette* and eventually becoming his American publisher and friend. In preaching about the "new birth" Whitefield was breaking down denominational barriers. This egalitarian "born-again" faith fit well with the American character, because it supported the idea that different denominations could coexist and respect one another, that their similarities were more important than their differences.

The historic tour of the colonies that Whitefield now undertook involved his traveling two thousand miles on horseback, and his ride from New York to Charleston was at that time the longest such ever undertaken in North America by a white man. Whitefield was an adept rider and far preferred riding his own horse to being drawn in a carriage or coach, whose bumpiness he found extremely disagreeable. In addition, Whitefield also traveled three thousand miles by boat during his American visit. He would officially preach 350 times and gave many smaller exhortations and talks to other smaller groups. Before he left America in January 1741, he had visited over seventy-five cities and towns, and everywhere he went the message was the same—that people must choose to be "born again" and must accept their new identity in Christ. Because Presbyterians and Congregationalists and Quakers and Baptists and others all heard the same message and all were free to respond similarly, Americans were becoming united in the wake of his nonstop preaching. People were being offered a new identity that fit well with the American way of thinking. Some were German by background and some were French and some were English, but none of it mattered: They were all equal under God; they were all Americans. This was something new, an identity that was separate from one's ethnicity or one's denomination. To be an American meant to buy into a new set of ideas about one's equal status in God's eyes—and by dint of this to be accepted into a new community, to be an American.

We must remember that in the 1730s, just before White-field's arrival in America, there had been a great revival in the area of Northampton, Massachusetts, fueled by the preaching of Jonathan Edwards. By 1740 this religious ardor had cooled somewhat, but when Whitefield visited, the banked fires flared up again and what had grown dormant was revived afresh. Edwards's wife, Sarah, wrote:

> *He is a born orator. You have already heard of his deep-toned, yet clear and melodious voice. O it is perfect music to listen to that alone! . . . You remember that David Hume thought it worth going 20 miles to hear him speak; and Garrick said, "He could move men to tears . . . in pronouncing the word Mesopotamia." . . . It is truly wonderful to see what a spell this preacher often casts over an audience by proclaiming the simplest truths of the Bible.*
>
> *. . . A prejudiced person, I know, might say that this is all theatrical artifice and display; but not so will anyone think who has seen and known him. He is a very devout and godly man, and his only aim seems to be to reach and influence men the best way. He speaks from the heart all aglow with love, and pours out a torrent of eloquence which is almost irresistible.*

From Northampton Whitefield traveled south along the Connecticut River valley toward Hartford. The almost inconceivable effects of his progress through the colonies during this time may be glimpsed in an extraordinary firsthand account left to us by Nathan Cole, a farmer and carpenter in Middletown, Connecticut:

> Now it pleased God to send Mr. Whitefield into this land; and my hearing of his preaching at Philadelphia, like one of the Old apostles, and many thousands flocking to hear him preach the Gospel, and great numbers were converted to Christ; I felt the Spirit of God drawing me by conviction, longed to see and hear him, and wished he would come this way. And I soon heard he was come to New York and the Jerseys and great multitudes flocking after him under great concern for their Souls and many converted which brought on my concern more and more hoping soon to see him but next I heard he was at Long Island, then at Boston, and next at Northampton.
>
> Then one morning all on a sudden, about 8 or 9 o'clock there came a messenger and said Mr. Whitefield preached at Hartford and Weathersfield yesterday and is to preach at Middletown this morning [October 23, 1740] at ten of the Clock. I was in my field at Work. I dropt my tool that I had in my hand and ran home and run through my house and bade my wife get ready quick to go and hear Mr. Whitefield preach at Middletown, and run to my pasture for my horse with all my might fearing that I

*should be too late to hear him. I brought my horse home
and soon mounted and took my wife up and went forward
as fast as I thought the horse could bear, and when my
horse began to be out of breath, I would get down and put
my wife on the Saddle and bid her ride as fast as she could
and not stop or slack for me except I bade her, and so I
would run until I was much out of breath, and then mount
my horse again, and so I did several times to favour my
horse, we improved every moment to get along as if we
were fleeing for our lives, all the while fearing we should
be too late to hear the Sermon, for we had twelve miles to
ride double in little more than an hour....*

*And when we came within about half a mile of the
road that comes down from Hartford Weathersfield and
Stepney to Middletown; on high land I saw before me a
Cloud or fogg rising. I first thought it came from the great
river [Connecticut River], but as I came nearer the Road,
I heard a noise something like a low rumbling thunder
and presently found it was the noise of horses feet coming
down the road and this Cloud was a Cloud of dust made
by the Horses feet. It arose some Rods into the air over the
tops of the hills and trees and when I came within about
20 rods of the Road, I could see men and horses slipping
along in the Cloud like shadows, and as I drew nearer it
seemed like a steady stream of horses and their riders,
scarcely a horse more than his length behind another, all*

of a lather and foam with sweat, their breath rolling out of their nostrils in the cloud of dust every jump; every horse seemed to go with all his might to carry his rider to hear news from heaven for the saving of Souls. It made me tremble to see the sight, how the world was in a struggle, I found a vacancy between two horses to slip in my horse; and my wife said law our clothes will be all spoiled see how they look, for they were so covered with dust, that they looked almost all of a colour coats, hats, and shirts and horses.

We went down in the stream; I heard no man speak a word all the way three miles but every one pressing forward in great haste and when we got to the old meeting house there was a great multitude; it was said to be 3 or 4000 of people assembled together, we got off from our horses and shook off the dust, and the ministers were then coming to the meeting house. I turned and looked towards the great river and saw the ferry boats running swift forward and forward bringing over loads of people; the oars rowed nimble and quick, every thing men horses and boats seemed to be struggling for life; the land and banks over the river looked black with people and horses all along the 12 miles. I saw no man at work in his field, but all seemed to be gone.

When I saw Mr. Whitefield come upon the scaffold he looked almost angelical, a young, slim slender youth be-

fore some thousands of people with a bold undaunted countenance, and my hearing how God was with him every where as he came along it solemnized my mind, and put me into a trembling fear before he began to preach; for he looked as if he was clothed with authority from the Great God, and a sweet solemn solemnity sat upon his brow. And my hearing him preach gave me a heart wound; by God's blessing my old foundation was broken up, and I saw that my righteousness would not save me.

That what Whitefield set in motion has come to be known as the Great Awakening can hardly surprise us. For wherever he went—and he went everywhere—he preached and preached. And wherever he preached hundreds and thousands like Nathan Cole came straggling to hear him and were changed by what he said. But it was not a mere mental assent to some theological doctrine. Many, like Benjamin Franklin, observed that people's behavior changed. Church rolls swelled and those who had merely been filling pews on Sunday suddenly understood why they were there. The Gospel came alive to them and they to it; and their common faith in God became the central animating force of the thirteen colonies that would in a few decades become the United States of America. William Cooper, a prominent Boston minister, hailed Whitefield as "the wonder of the age."

To be clear, Whitefield's preaching had an effect in Great Britain too, and dramatically opened the door for the efforts of the Wesleys and the Methodist movement in general, which led to many social reforms, not least through the efforts of William Wilberforce and the Clapham Circle, as we shall see. And it also helped lead the people of Great Britain along the path toward greater democratization. But all of this simply could not compare with the effects of his preaching in the American colonies.

In the American colonies, for reasons I have touched upon, the stage was set for a historic eruption such as never had been seen before or since. For one thing, the American people were part of a culture that was already far more deeply based in the Christian faith than its European counterparts. That many had traveled there for religious freedom was a large part of that. Also, in part because of their distance from the mother country, the Americans had almost been governing themselves already. But the advent of Whitefield and the Great Awakening would strengthen these inclinations dramatically and would put forward additional ideas that had never been considered. For one thing, the idea that everyone could have a direct relationship with God and that all were equal before God led to the idea that earthly authorities could be judged and should be judged. If God was the ultimate judge and the Judge above all other judges, then surely each person could consider whether those in authority over him were exercising that authority in accordance with God's principles—or not in accordance with God's principles, which is to say, in a way that could be considered tyrannous. This was an unprecedented development.

So Whitefield's preaching greatly tempered people's fear of authority and strengthened the native suspicion of authority, which went a long way toward solidifying what we today see as the American character.

But it wasn't merely that the American colonists became more religious and therefore more capable of—and inclined toward—self-government. The very message of Whitefield's preaching was itself inclined toward the ideas of liberty and self-government. By making each person see that God wished to have a direct relationship with every one of his children, no matter their social standing, the church authorities were effectively cut out of the equation. There was something empowering about knowing that one could go directly to God, and it introduced what we may think of as a free market of ideas into the situation. Each person could choose for himself what church he thought best and what preachers or teachers he thought most closely adhered to the theology that Whitefield had put forth. And there were many options to choose from, chiefly because Whitefield's success as he traveled throughout the colonies had spawned a host of imitators who themselves set out to preach in the great homiletic vacuum created by his wake.

Wherever one hailed from, whatever church one belonged to, whatever birth one might claim, or social rank, all were equal in God's sight. Furthermore, someone who might be outwardly common could know that all of God's children were the children of the sovereign of the universe, so they too were members of the only royal family that mattered, because the Scriptures said they were members of a "royal priesthood."

The most august dukes and earls were sinners who could be saved only by grace, the very same grace that saved the commonest commoner. The Gospel of Christ was the most powerful sociological leveler in history, and although the message had existed for seventeen centuries, it would burst into full bloom only now—at this crucial point in history—under the watering can of Whitefield's preaching. And over the decades this changed the colonies and created an American people.

The egalitarian strains of the Gospel extended to women and blacks as well. Many female preachers were spawned by the revival of the Great Awakening and many African American preachers too. Unlike most of the mainline ministers of his day, Whitefield often spoke to "Negroes" and once remarked that he was especially touched when one of them came to faith. One of them even asked Whitefield, "Have I a soul?" That Whitefield believed he did meant that the Negro was in this most important respect perfectly equal to whites.

Whitefield's preaching was a great social leveler throughout the colonies. But it was a great uniter of the people in the colonies too. By the time Whitefield died in 1770, an inconceivable 80 percent of the population of the American colonies had heard him preach at least once. By traveling as he did, he accomplished what no one else had ever done. He became known to all in the colonies equally. He was the first American celebrity, but he was much more than a mere celebrity.

The Reverend John Piper reminds us that before "Whitefield there was no unifying inter-colonial person or event" and "before Whitefield, it is doubtful any name other than royalty was known equally from Boston to Charleston." So his impact on the culture and thinking of early and mideighteenth-century America can hardly be overstated. Piper says that "by 1750 virtually every American loved and admired Whitefield and saw him as their champion."

For example, while not brazenly antiestablishment, Whitefield often and openly criticized ministers and pastors whom he thought merely going through the motions and not living out the kind of real and vibrant faith he preached about. They were not only not "saved" but also guilty of preventing their parishioners from finding God, "the blind leading the blind." Such sentiments did not sit well with the authorities, but Whitefield was not cowed by their threats and even crossed swords with bishops in the Church of England. So to the common man who saw the church as a mere extension of the oppressive power of the state, Whitefield was a hero.

He united the colonies as they had never been united, articulating what they came to believe. So that everyone who accepted these views about liberty and independence—with all of their ramifications and corollaries—would have this in common with the others who did; and sharing these ideas set forth by Whitefield became a vital part of what it meant to be an American. All who believed these things began to think of themselves as Americans as much as—if not more than—they thought of themselves as citizens of Connecticut or Maryland or North Carolina, for example. The various members of the thirteen colonies thus slowly became a people; and these people—this people—would eventually seek political independence and would become a nation.

George Whitefield has been called the spiritual founding father of the United States. His travel and the effects of his travel went far beyond the American colonies. He traveled to preach in Scotland fifteen times, twice to Ireland, and preached in the Netherlands, Gibraltar, and Bermuda too; and shortly after his death Augustus Montague Toplady, author of the famous hymn "Rock of Ages," deemed him "the apostle of the English empire." But nothing can begin to touch the effect of his preaching in the American colonies. After the revolution had begun, he was seen as something like a patron saint, the Protestant American saint of the cause. Indeed, he was buried in Northburyport, Massachusetts, and for many years his corpse was exposed so that devotees who had journeyed to his tomb could gaze upon his mouldering remains. Before becoming an eponymous turncoat, Benedict Arnold on his way to seize Quebec, made a pilgrimage to the grave of Whitefield and himself cut off a small piece of the great man's clothing as a relic.

When we take the full measure of Whitefield's role in creating what would become the United States, who can help but wonder whether our history is one in which God himself—and if not God, then at least those who are motivated by the idea of God and all it portends—has played a central role? There is no question that after Whitefield's decades among us the stage was set for the next act in the story of this people. Among other things, they had in common a suspicious view of authority and a particular revulsion of tyranny, and they were now ready to stand up to the aggressions of the mother country, even to take up arms, if necessary, and to become something entirely new in the history of the world. The colonies were united as they never had been before, and their citizens had a far deeper sense of the rightness of self-government and liberty than before, and of the central role of faith in living that out.

FOUR

Venerating Our Heroes

I have said that it is important for citizens to behave morally in order for self-government to work. But as I also have said, self-government entails far more than obeying laws. Tocqueville refers to what he calls the "habits of the heart" and the "mores" of the American people. He says that it is these things that are really at the center of keeping our republic. Going to church and obeying laws are important, but there are other things that also deserve to be mentioned and examined as central to keeping our freedoms. In talking about all of these things, whether about having faith or going to church or being law-abiding, we need to keep in mind that all of these things reinforce one another. We cannot pretend that one or another of these is alone sufficient. They are all part of the larger secret formula. They're all part of a larger mind-set. But right now let's look at one of them, what we will call the veneration of heroes.

In talking about that we are really talking about an appreciation for and celebration of the heroic in general. And as I will explain, this is something that has fallen far out of favor in our nation, to our deepest detriment. As the author of biographies of great men and women I have seen firsthand just how deeply encouraging and inspiring the stories of heroes can be. There seems to be something within the human breast that naturally responds to such stories, that positively longs for them. For some reason having to do with our nature, heroic examples call forth from us a powerful desire to be good and great and heroic ourselves. This should hardly surprise us. As far back as *Plutarch's Lives*, written in the first century, we have many books telling the stories of great individuals; and these books have had the express purpose of inspiring others to similar greatness. In fact, *Plutarch's Lives* was the book one of my own heroes, Dietrich Bonhoeffer, was reading in his last days.

But just as we seem in the last fifty years to have misunderstood or forgotten entirely the role that faith and virtue have in our republic, so we seem also to have abandoned the vital tradition of venerating heroes. It is a shocking departure from a nearly universal cultural norm, one found in almost all cultures, with every kind of government. If we are to keep the republic, we must again seriously consider this absolutely vital tradition.

One dramatic example of the change from understanding this idea to failing to do so is obvious to me whenever I run through Central Park here in Manhattan, where I live. Created in the 1850s by Frederick Law Olmsted and Calvert Vaux, Central Park is nearly everywhere throughout its verdant 843 acres festooned with heroic statues and busts, most from the nineteenth century. One especially prominent example is the statue of Daniel Webster, whose bronze figure glowers from atop an imposing granite plinth near 72nd Street. There are two statues of Christopher Columbus, one in which he is nobly looking upward to God, in obvious thanks for allowing him the privilege of having sailed to the New World.

On Literary Walk there are statues of Shakespeare, Robert Burns, and Sir Walter Scott, and nearby are busts of Beethoven and Schiller. Near Fifth Avenue there is a statue of the inventor Samuel Morse, who was friends with another of my heroes, William Wilberforce, and by Turtle Pond stands the largest of all the statues in the park, an equestrian statue of King Jagiełło of Poland, given in 1945. There is also a statue of Simón Bolívar and one of the German naturalist Alexander von Humboldt. I almost daily run past a noble gray stone statue of Alexander Hamilton just south of the reservoir. But in recent years this tradition of heroic statuary has vanished. The last oversized statue of a historic figure is one of Hans Christian Andersen, dedicated in 1959, but he is situated not heroically but rather humbly, at ground level. In fact, he is seated, a welcoming, genial giant obviously meant for children to clamber over, as they do. He is heartwarming and unthreatening, but he is certainly not inspiring or heroic. The era of such figures in our public statuary had passed.

One might object that in 1994 a statue was put up of the founder of the New York City Marathon, Fred Lebow, but it's a far cry from the heroic figures throughout the rest of the park. For one thing, it's only life-sized and Lebow was a small man. For another, it's nearly at ground level. You don't look up at him, you walk up to him as though he were an actual man standing there, and he won't look back, because in decidedly unheroic fashion he's looking at his watch. His other hand is on his hip. The point, of course, is to say that he was an ordinary man, a man of the people, a man too busy with living his life to be venerated. The statue isn't disrespectful of him at all, but all told, it has far more in common with a mannequin than with anything of a heroic nature.

So what has happened? Since roughly the 1960s, public expressions of the heroic, whether in stories or other artworks, have effectively disappeared. America decided that it made more sense to be suspicious of heroes than to venerate them. The lessons of the Vietnam War and Watergate sent the general message that we shouldn't trust our leaders and that our previous trust in them had been largely misplaced. The slogan

"Question Authority" suddenly bloomed everywhere, and even that imperative seemed less to mean that we should rightly question authority to determine whether it was legitimate than to question the idea of authority altogether, as though all authority and truth claims were the cynical schemes of old men clinging to power. A kind of forced egalitarianism made its way into the culture and has been with us ever since. Venerating heroes is generally not something we do much anymore, if at all. It's become mostly fashionable either to ignore them or to denigrate them for their faults. We think, for example, of George Washington not as heroically standing in the prow of the boat crossing the Delaware and who made tremendous personal sacrifices to help establish the United States, but as someone who owned slaves. Regarding him as an extraordinary champion of freedom and liberty is little anymore done. He is now thought of far less as a hero to be venerated than as a hypocrite to be openly vilified or as someone simply stupidly indifferent to the suffering of his slaves and therefore to be politely or pointedly ignored.

Of course it's true that people can venerate heroes so much that they overlook important flaws. For example, once we know that JFK routinely had prostitutes brought to him in the White House it becomes difficult to venerate him as any kind of noble leader. And there are times when, in an effort to venerate mythic heroes, we go too far and present them as almost magical figures; for example, St. Patrick is thought of less as a profoundly courageous missionary to the pagan Irish tribes than as a mystical sprite who drove the snakes out of Ireland.

Most have felt that the veneration of George Washington by Parson Weems went much too far in the direction of hagiography, portraying Washington more as a deity—in the way the Romans portrayed their emperors as deities. Weems is the man who wrote a very popular book called *The Life of Washington* in 1800, the year after Washington's death. In it he makes several claims that seem at least partly far-fetched, such as that at age six Washington chopped down a cherry tree and then promptly owned up to it with the now-famous phrase "I cannot tell a lie." This and other stories were picked up by the ubiquitous *McGuffey Reader* and spread throughout nineteenth-century America as facts. So the idea that some corrective was in order is nothing to be dismissed. Still, the claim that Washington chopped down a cherry tree and said what is reported in Weems's book has never been proved untrue either. Washington's relatives maintained that it was indeed true. And most of what is said about him and his heroic exploits is true. He had many horses shot out from under him during his daring military leadership in the French and Indian War and is widely recorded to have been physically brave and profoundly inspiring to the men under him. That he didn't hurl a silver dollar across the Potomac or sport a set of wooden teeth is ultimately beside the point. He was, by any fair historical index, an extraordinary and virtuous and noble figure.

In any case, in latter decades we have swung so far in the other direction that venerating heroes, which used to be part of our common vocabulary, is no longer a language we speak or really understand. But this has served to undermine the very idea of greatness and the idea of the heroic, which is deeply destructive to any culture but especially to a free society like ours, where aspiring to be like the heroes who have gone before us is a large part of what makes citizens want to behave admirably. Denigrating heroes, or simply failing to venerate them, has a cynical and toxic effect on the young generation, and we have now had fifty years in which we have neglected this "habit of the heart" so vital to our free way of life.

NATHAN HALE

As if to illustrate my point, during the writing of this book Yale's alumni magazine arrived in my mailbox with a headline about Nathan Hale on the cover: NATHAN HALE AS YOU'VE NEVER SEEN HIM BEFORE. I'd been reading about him and realized how little one hears of him anymore, and I realized that this was part of this larger trend. In a way, Hale was the very first American hero. All contemporary descriptions of him give us a picture of someone who might have been portrayed by a very young Henry Fonda. Tall and good-looking, known for his fun-loving spirit as well as for his devout Christian faith, Hale seems to have been someone who really had a heroic bearing in life, even before his capture by the British. But it is the end of his life—his boldly volunteering to go behind British lines for his own hero, George Washington, his subsequent capture, and his noble composure as he was hanged—that forms the essence of his legend.

Immediately after his death, word spread among the soldiers and citizenry of how he had died and of his now-famous words as he stood there, about to step into eternity: "My only regret is that I have but one life to give for my country." Though the precise words are argued about, there is little doubt he expressed the noble sentiment. Two ballads about him were soon written, one of them by someone who knew him well, and these ballads were circulated among the soldiers of Washington's army. The idea was that this first-acknowledged hero of the Continental Army must be remembered, and not just for his own sake but for theirs. His bravery in life and his patriotic courage in facing death must be memorialized so that others could be inspired by it. Because they would need to be in the trials that lay ahead. And who can doubt that many who heard those ballads recited or sung were indeed inspired by them, by Hale's example? That was why the ballads were written and it has been one of the vital roles that art has always played in our national life, indeed in the life of almost every nation and culture.

In fact, in 1914, while the world was descending into the First World War, a magnificent statue of Hale was dedicated outside Connecticut Hall, the very dorm he had inhabited on Yale's Old

Campus. The Georgian brick building was built in 1753 and still stands there. It is where he slept and studied Hebrew and where he argued and laughed with his fellow classmates. And in the grand tradition of memorializing the great, the famous artist Bela Lyon Pratt, himself a Yale graduate, was in 1912 commissioned to create the sculpture. He was at that time one of the nation's most highly regarded sculptors, who along with his mentor, Augustus Saint-Gaudens, was given the highest honor of having his work used on the golden U.S. coinage of the time. Lyon's statue of Hale is a masterpiece, perfectly capturing the nobility of that young hero in the very moment of his tragic triumph. A copy of the statue, dedicated in 1948, also stands in front of the Department of Justice in Washington, DC. Another stands at Fort Nathan Hale in Connecticut, and another in front of Tribune Tower in Chicago. The base of the statue is inscribed with these words:

NATHAN HALE
CAPTAIN
ARMY OF THE UNITED STATES
BORN AT COVENTRY CONNECTICUT
JUNE 6, 1755
    IN THE PERFORMANCE OF HIS
    DUTY HE RESIGNED HIS
    LIFE A SACRIFICE TO
    HIS COUNTRY'S LIBERTY
    AT NEW YORK

SEPTEMBER 22, 1776

When I saw my alumni magazine, I remembered the glorious statue of Hale on Old Campus and excitedly flipped to the article, only to be greeted by a bizarre and disturbing picture. It was of a Nathan Hale bobblehead doll, carefully fashioned to mimic the statue, except, of course for the goofy oversized head on a spring, made the more ridiculous by the serious expression on it. The short article cheerfully explained that the grotesque curio had been created by the class of 1975 as a clever giveaway for their fortieth reunion. I could hardly believe what I was reading and seeing. Who could have thought it a good idea to design and manufacture a bobblehead doll of this hero of American liberty, this young patriot of patriots, brutally hanged by the British in the bloom of his youth? The Pratt statue on Old Campus—and this bobblehead version of the statue—depicts him in the moment of his execution, facing death bravely. His hands are bound behind his back and his feet are bound. It is the sacred moment when he faced eternity.

History tells us that the handsome, pious twenty-one-year-old acted so nobly that many around him on the British side were deeply affected, that some were horrified that this gentle soul should be executed. But the man in charge of the execution was of another opinion. He was a hardened soldier who relished the idea of making an example of this handsome traitor who had dared spy for that foulest of all foul traitors, George Washington. Hale was hanged from a tree in an orchard near what is today East 63rd Street in Manhattan, less than half a mile from where I write. Though it's almost inconceivable in our time, this area was all farmland and orchards. We know that the officer ordered that Hale's body be left hanging from the tree, so that he would be deliberately denied a Christian burial and his family would never recover what was left of his remains. Animals and insects would feed on his body and birds would peck at his eyes.

The contemptuous British officer's mockery and desecration of the man they accused of spying was vicious and deliberate, and no doubt stories of it would have rallied his fellow soldiers to fight the hated British all the harder, to avenge this foul injustice. And of course, Hale's mockery and desecration at the hands of the Yale class of 1975 was not vicious or deliberate. It was meant to be arch and clever, and in a letter to the editor answering my criticism of it the word "whimsical" was used. The idea, of course, is that anyone who would object to this simply must not understand whimsy and must not understand that those behind this idea were not thinking of Hale's martyrdom to American liberty. As far as the members of the class of 1975 were concerned, he was just an overly serious and somber bronze figure stationed outside the dorm where they had spent their rollicksome freshman year. To think deeply about him was certainly never the point of creating their *outré* memento, which is, of course, exactly my point in bringing up the subject. How is it possible that we can have drifted to this point, where the hanging death of a young man who fought to defend the very liberties we enjoy now—even in the very act of treating his memory this way—should be so thoroughly forgotten that even the statue erected so that he would be remembered would be insufficient in helping us remember him, so that even in remembering that statue we would forget why it should be remembered?

That statue was put there to help Americans—and young Yale men in particular—to think of the heroic sacrifices that had been made for them, so that they would be grateful for those sacrifices and so that they would themselves be inspired to similar sacrifices. In fact, three years after the statue was erected, young Americans, many of them Yale men, were called up to serve their country in the First World War, and for most of them the statue would have served as an inspiration. The existence of a photograph from around 1918 of two Yalies dressed in their doughboy uniforms and proudly flanking the statue makes that movingly clear.

It seems obvious that however we have come to this place, we must acknowledge where we are and consider the ramifications, which are dire, and must quickly do all we can to remedy the situation. The first thing we can do we are doing now: We are acknowledging it and discussing it. And we must understand that it is only in the last fifty years that this has changed. Throughout our history, our greatest artists have played a role in rousing us to think of the greatness of our nation and of its heroes, often with the very purpose of exhorting us to fight for our liberties when they were threatened.

In the First World War there were innumerable popular songs, such as "Over There," written toward that end. And in World War II many movies were made with the simple idea of rallying the nation to the fight. Not all of them depicted the lives of heroes, but all of them were heroic. One that did depict the life of a hero was the story of Sergeant York, played in the eponymously named film by Gary Cooper. In life, York had been a deeply religious young man who seriously questioned whether it was right to fight in the war. In a scene in the film he is praying for an answer to his dilemma when the pages of his Bible are riffled by the wind and his eyes seem to light providentially on Jesus's injunction that we are to "render unto Caesar the things that are Caesar's and unto God the things that are God's." So off he went to sign up. His exploits on the battlefield were so selfless and spectacular that after seeing them depicted in the theater, many young men marched straight to the recruitment office to sign up. Heroes inspire us, and whenever our nation has faced a crisis, it has fallen to poets and sculptors and painters and songwriters, and later to filmmakers too, to rally the nation to its feet, to inspire the young men and women of the nation to do what they must. Churchill's wartime speeches may, of course, be seen as a form of this too. Their supreme artfulness and the artfulness of his delivery may well have made the difference between losing and winning the war against Hitler and the Nazis. So the art of creating heroic and inspiring art has played a vital role in the history of the world and the wars of this world, and in the grander battle between good and evil.

All of which brings me to the story of Paul Revere.

PAUL REVERE'S RIDE

When my daughter was seven, I was reading through the Dover Books catalog to find a Christmas present for her. In so doing, I spotted something that captured my fancy as few things ever have. It read: "Cut & Assemble the Paul Revere House. An H.O. Scale Model in Full Color by Edmund V. Gillon, Jr." Something about this, and about doing this together with my daughter powerfully appealed to me, so I ordered it. When it arrived, I began the slow process of carefully cutting out the various pieces with an X-acto knife and then painstakingly folding and gluing them together with her, until—lo and behold!—we at last had a tiny replica of Paul Revere's house in the North End of Boston.

What was it about that diminutive structure that entranced me so? Somehow the smallness of it was a factor, which reminds me of that passage in C. S. Lewis's memoir *Surprised by Joy* in which he remembers as a child being transported by the diminutive garden his brother Warnie had fashioned from moss and twigs in the upturned rectangle of an old cookie tin lid. What is it about the elfin magic of things miniature? But that's another subject for another time. The model paper house somehow drew me into the story of Paul Revere and his era, and before you could say "The British are coming!" I found myself for the first time reading Henry Wadsworth Longfellow's famous poem "Paul Revere's Ride."

I'd heard snippets of it throughout my life, as everyone has, but I was sort of amazed I'd never actually read it all the way through, just as I had been amazed I had no familiarity with what Os Guinness calls the Golden Triangle of Freedom. How had this extraordinary poem escaped me? It was longer than I thought, and it began with the familiar lines I'd heard many times:

> *Listen, my children, and you shall hear*
> *Of the midnight ride of Paul Revere.*
> *On the eighteenth of April, in Seventy-Five;*
> *Hardly a man is now alive*
> *Who remembers that famous day and year.*

As I continued reading I was startled by how good it was. It was spectacular. Why had I thought otherwise? The simple answer is that as an English major at Yale and in the cultural circles I frequented afterward, the poet and his popular ilk were sneered at, much as Norman Rockwell's superb illustrations were sneered at. Their shared crime was being accessible and popular, because somehow in the twentieth century difficulty and obscurity had become artistic virtues, such that the impenetrable brake of *Finnegans Wake* and the actively drab daubings of Robert Motherwell had become revered and celebrated. What's more, Longfellow's great poem, like most popular poetry, rhymed, which in the pretentious precincts of twentieth-century letters was thought impossibly vulgar.

But since I was two decades removed from the milieu in which these ideas about poetry were promoted, I was free to enjoy it as a child might have done, and as its first readers did, many of whom were, of course, children. And as I read it I was utterly mesmerized. I didn't wonder that many generations of schoolchildren had been required to memorize it and that they remembered much of it into their old age. It was simply that good and now, all these years later, I had discovered it too.

But how had I grown up in a world that no longer valued this great treasure? Of course, we have discussed that in part already, but reading Longfellow's poem was one of the first times I had been truly bowled over by how different our country was now that we didn't value such things and didn't celebrate mythic heroes like Paul Revere. The reality of our poverty on this score struck me with force.

It was one of the reasons I began thinking about writing this book. I realized that by ceasing to tell these mythic and heroic stories of our history, we had in fact lost touch with ourselves, and in a way that would be suicidal if we didn't do something about it. After all, if we don't know the stories of America, how can we know America? We are more than political ideas. We are a people who live those ideas out in common. Knowing those ideas is a vital first step, but part of how we know them is knowing how they came into being and how they were subsequently lived out in history. So by pushing away these common stories of our heroes, we have allowed ourselves to be drained of our very common identity as Americans. Our emotions must be as engaged in "keeping" the republic as our minds are engaged in it. It is the real stories of heroes like Washington and Nathan Hale and others that help us to properly feel the power of the ideas behind them. We must feel the horror of tyranny and must love the noble idea of liberty. We must love America.

We cannot reduce things to the intellectual. In the end we must feel those ideas and see them embodied in heroes and stories. By deciding that every potential hero is too flawed to celebrate and venerate, or that such stories are somehow corny, we have done a grave disservice to several generations and to the country. We've not only denied our citizens the inspirational stories of those who have made great sacrifices from which we benefit but have also denied several generations the knowledge of what it really means to be an American—and we have denied them the appropriate sense of patriotism that everyone longs to feel. Love of one's country is among the fundamental joys of what it means to be human.

Unless we celebrate our common ideals and stories—and our common story—and unless we are unified in celebrating those things, we can never appreciate who we are and what we have. If we don't feel the power of what has gone before, we will hardly be drawn to do our part in perpetuating American liberty. That's what songs and poems and stories and paintings and sculptures can do. So already to the extent that we have ceased hearing and memorizing poems like Longfellow's poem about Paul Revere, we have in some terrible sense ceased to be America. By drifting along for half a century as our common stories and heroes have faded or been pushed away, we have increasingly become America in name only. And we haven't even realized it.

To the extent that we are in such a place already, we are already living on borrowed time, like a cut flower that still appears fresh and beautiful but that, because it's been separated from the source of its life, has begun to die. America, that great and fragile experiment in liberty, has become cut off from its roots. We need to see this and we need to do all we can to remedy it, and quickly.

⸻

Let's go back to Longfellow's poem. I remember that as I read through its magnificent lines, its peculiar magic worked on me.

For the first time in my life I found myself seriously thinking about the dangers faced and being moved emotionally by the great sacrifices of those in the revolutionary era. I was disturbed to think that this had never been brought home to me before. And I realized that by the time I was a student at Yale, the heroic and patriotic were actively ridiculed. The idea of loving one's country was thought hopelessly backward and even offensive.

But as I read the Longfellow poem now, as an adult, I saw that we had done something deeply regrettable. The feelings I felt reading it were the same feelings millions of parents and teachers and schoolchildren had felt over many generations, but very few in my generation or the generations that followed had experienced that. The idea of loving one's country had been forgotten, and very few people any longer knew these stories or had the joy of knowing the poem's great lines.

But before I say more about Longfellow's great poem specifically, let's refresh our memories about what led to the events it describes.

THE ROAD TO PAUL REVERE

Paul Revere's ride took place at the dawn of the American Revolution. Actually, it took place just a few hours before the battles at Lexington and Concord. In fact, following his ride through the night, Revere himself witnessed the violence at Lexington.

But let's scroll back to what led up to that, and to the subsequent conflict known as the War of Independence.

As I said in the previous chapters, America was by the 1770s more attuned to the ideas of liberty and self-government than they had been forty years earlier, and more inclined to want to throw off what they increasingly saw as the tyrannical government of the British. But the tensions between Great Britain and her American colonies began in earnest immediately after the French and Indian War (1754–63). The British, having nearly doubled their national debt in fighting that war, decided to levy heavy new taxes on the colonists. The Americans thought the taxes severe, especially because they had no political power themselves—which is to say, no representation in Parliament—so in response to what they felt an undue and unfair burden, they began to offer resistance and generally to express their growing discontent more openly.

In December 1773 they expressed their discontent dramatically, in what came to be called the Boston Tea Party, in which a group of Boston's rebel leaders boarded a merchant vessel in Boston Harbor and destroyed its extremely valuable cargo of tea. Many of those involved were dressed as Mohawk Indians, to pointedly express their allegiance to America. In response, the British immediately imposed harsh punitive measures on the colonists, which came to be known as the Intolerable Acts. But rather than breaking the will of the Americans, they served only to inflame things further and to recruit many more to the cause of liberty.

By February 1775 things had become so unmanageable that the British declared Boston to be in a state of rebellion. The Sons of Liberty—which was the name the colonial rebel leaders had given themselves—had been preparing for possible armed conflict with the British for some time, storing ammunition and weapons in the area. Several times the British discovered the caches and confiscated them, but the Sons of Liberty eventually developed a spy network that allowed them to stay one step ahead of their enemies.

A number of their couriers often rode great distances to relay messages. One of them was a successful forty-year-old Boston silversmith and engraver named Paul Revere. History records at least eighteen such journeys for Revere, including one of nearly sixty miles to Portsmouth, New Hampshire, another of over two hundred miles to Manhattan, and another of three hundred miles to Philadelphia.

But it was for a shorter ride that Revere has become famous.

Intelligence had revealed that the British planned to march toward Lexington and Concord in the wee hours of April 18 with plans to arrest two of the lead troublemakers, John Hancock and Samuel Adams. Adams was the fiery founder of the Sons of Liberty while Hancock's defiance was such that a year later his name would famously become synonymous with one's signature. The colonists already knew their two leaders would likely be arrested soon, so Adams and Hancock hid that night in the home of one of Hancock's relatives in Lexington.[1]

The Sons of Liberty had worked out several methods of staying a step ahead of the British. One was to have two riders travel to Lexington and Concord via different routes, so if one was captured the other would still get the message through. One courier would ride from Boston while the other would cross the Charles River and be waiting to ride from Charleston. But how to get the message to the second rider? Paul Revere met with the sexton of the Old North Church and arranged that lanterns would be carried to the top of the steeple and lit as a signal. Rising to a dizzying 191 feet, the magnificent steeple of the Old North Church was the highest point in Boston. If one lantern was lit, the Charleston rider would know the British were riding via land; two would signal that the British had chosen to cross the river first and ride along another somewhat shorter route.

On the night of April 18, Revere himself was the one chosen to cross Boston Harbor to Charleston, there to await the signal from the Old North Church; and another rider, William Dawes, would depart directly from Boston. When the Sons of Liberty knew the British were indeed mustering their troops for the journey, Dawes and Revere were dispatched. The British had elected to ferry their troops across the river before marching them to Concord, so it was in fact two lanterns that shone that night from the steeple of the Old North Church.

As they rode along their separate routes, Dawes and Revere warned all the rebels they could along the way, who would in turn tell others, so about forty riders in total fanned out that night to ride throughout Middlesex County. Because he had departed from Charleston, Revere arrived in Lexington around midnight to warn Hancock and Adams. Dawes, taking the longer route, arrived a half hour later. Once they'd been warned, Hancock and Adams planned to sneak off to the town of Burlington, five and a half miles north. Dawes and Revere continued toward Concord, warning still others along their route. They were joined on this last leg by a third rider, Dr. Samuel Prescott. But the three of them got only as far as the town of Lincoln before a British army patrol stopped them. Prescott jumped his horse over a wall and escaped into the woods, and Dawes escaped too. But Revere was captured and questioned at gunpoint, after which he was marched with other rebel captives back toward Lexington.

When they were about a half mile from the town, a shot was heard and then a church bell began to toll. The British, discovering that this meant the colonists were mustering to fight, released their captives and returned to their commanders. But they confiscated Revere's horse, so he walked to Lexington, where at daybreak with his own eyes he witnessed the last part of the first battle in the great war for American independence.

But in the decades after, history mostly forgot about Paul Revere and his April 1775 ride through the night. He served in the war and afterward had an extraordinary career as an early industrialist, building a significant business that survives to this day as Revere Copper Products. But when Revere died in 1818, his obituary did not even make glancing mention of his heroic ride through the night on the eve of the War of Independence.

The only reason we know of him is because of another crisis in American history many years later, known to us as the Civil War.

Of course, in that second crisis the threat came not from our so-called mother country but from our own brothers to the south. The tension between the "slave states"—which hoped to secede from the Union—and the Northern states—which weren't inclined to let them, had been escalating dramatically. Just as conflict had seemed inevitable in 1775, so did it seem inevitable in 1860. The people of the latter era wondered whether this nation could survive. Would the people of the Northern states be up to what lay ahead?

That question was on the mind of one Northerner, the poet Henry Wadsworth Longfellow, an ardent abolitionist since 1842. Longfellow was friends with the famous abolitionist Charles Sumner, but it was sheer happenstance that almost certainly was the cause of what blossomed in his mind in April 1860 and would become the poem for which he is best known.[2]

Twenty-eight years before he thought of his poem about Paul Revere, one of Longfellow's earliest poems was published in the *New England Magazine.* The same issue of that magazine (October 1828) published a reprint of a written account of Paul Revere's ride that Revere himself had been asked to write back in 1797. There is little doubt that the young Longfellow read that rather obscure account of Revere's ride in the same issue of the *New England Magazine* containing his early poem, and that he remembered it all those years.

So in 1860 he recalled Paul Revere's obscure story, and it occurred to him that he should tell it in verse. He wished to write a poem that had a mythic and heroic quality, with the explicit intention of inspiring the people of his generation to face the crisis that loomed before them. He knew that just as everything had hung in the balance in 1775, it hung in the balance now. Perhaps a poetic retelling of Revere's heroic ride would make a difference. He knew that the American people needed to be moved emotionally to fight for what they knew was right, to fight against the injustice of slavery, and to fight to keep the republic.

At the suggestion of a friend, Longfellow on April 5 toured the old part of Boston. He visited Boston's Old North Church and climbed far up into the hallowed space of the tall steeple from which had shone those two lanterns all those years before.[3] The very next day Longfellow began work on his poem.

To inspire his fellow Americans he would appeal to their common history, to reach beyond the legalities of the Constitution to the very soul of America, to the common spirit of liberty whose flame shone so brightly on that morning after Revere's ride. There are some things that are beyond the reach of the law. The crisis that led this nation to civil war was one of them.

Longfellow felt that as a famous poet he had a duty to use his talents for his nation. He understood that every people needs myths and legends and heroes. He had written "The Song of Hiawatha" and "The Courtship of Miles Standish" for the same reason. Longfellow's magnificent poem did precisely what he had hoped: It created the legend of Paul Revere. It was published that December of 1860 in a new magazine called the *Atlantic Monthly*. We don't know what effect it had on those facing the Civil War, but we do know that in the decade following the war the poem grew in prominence, as did the story of Paul Revere's ride. Schoolchildren began memorizing it and reciting it at annual celebrations. In 1875 and 1876, at the nation's centennial, the poem enjoyed a particular surge of popularity. In 1883 a twenty-two-year-old sculptor, Cyrus Edwin Dallin, was commissioned to create a Paul Revere sculpture to stand in the plaza across from the Old North Church. His designs were not approved until 1899, and the sculpture itself was not unveiled until 1940, but ever since it has been one of the most popular and photographed tourist sites in Boston.

There is so much to admire in the poem and there is a reason it has lasted as it has. While the subjects and meters of Longfellow's other famous poems such as "The Song of Hiawatha" and "The Courtship of Miles Standish" can veer toward seeming pedantic or even lugubrious, there is something inescapably fresh and exciting about this unapologetic paean to

American liberty. There are many reasons it stood the test of time and appropriately excited the patriotism of generations of Americans, as we shall see.

The opening lines of the poem are, of course, the most familiar. They are powerfully evocative, signaling that we are about to hear something extraordinary and mythical:

> *Listen, my children, and you shall hear*
> *Of the midnight ride of Paul Revere,*
> *On the eighteenth of April, in Seventy-five;*
> *Hardly a man is now alive*
> *Who remembers that famous day and year.*

We all ask, "What famous day and year?" Our interest is already piqued, just as the poet intends, and we are drawn into the story immediately. Part of what makes the poem so particularly good is Longfellow's protean ability to dramatically vary the voice and mood of the poem from one stanza to the next. For example, when he writes of Revere's friend climbing the steeple of the Old North Church, the rhythm of the words feels like someone climbing haltingly.

> *Then he climbed the tower of the Old North Church,*
> *By the wooden stairs, with stealthy tread,*

To the belfry chamber overhead,
And startled the pigeons from their perch
On the sombre rafters, that round him made
Masses and moving shapes of shade,—

The reader can almost smell the dry wooden beams and feel the silence and dead air of that enclosed and lonely space. When he climbs to the very top, we can sense how impossibly high and solitary it must have felt to be so far above the slumbering and silent town, high up in the belfry.

By the trembling ladder, steep and tall,
To the highest window in the wall,
Where he paused to listen and look down
A moment on the roofs of the town
And the moonlight flowing over all.

Longfellow wants us to feel the eeriness of the aerie, to feel that we ourselves are up there, terribly alone. His use of the word *trembling* and the image of the moonlight create a sense of lonely fear that culminates in the next lines, with their deft use of the words *dead* and *spell* and *creeping* and *secret dread*. It's impossible not to note the sinister, gooseflesh-inducing macabreness of these syllables, worthy of the voice of an Orson Welles or a Vincent Price.

Beneath, in the churchyard, lay the dead,
In their night encampment on the hill,
Wrapped in silence so deep and still
That he could hear, like a sentinel's tread,
The watchful night-wind, as it went
Creeping along from tent to tent,
And seeming to whisper, "All is well!"
A moment only he feels the spell
Of the place and the hour, and the secret dread
Of the lonely belfry and the dead;

But just at the point when we might shriek, Longfellow gives us relief, instantly shifting the mood and focus to what the climber spies all the way in the distance across Boston Harbor; and suddenly we are safely far beyond the lonely belfry and again out—out in the exciting world of military maneuvers. Then again he shifts the focus to a close-up, as it were, of our hero, Paul Revere, impatiently fidgeting as he waits with his horse across the water, and then yet again he dramatically shifts the feeling to high excitement as Revere spies the *glimmer* and then the *gleam* of the lanterns' light and finally and forthwith literally leaps into action.

In the alliteration of the next four lines, and even more in their meter, Longfellow masterfully gives us the unmistakable feeling of a horse galloping with gathering speed and urgency into the blackness of the night:

A hurry of hoofs in a village street,
A shape in the moonlight, a bulk in the dark,
And beneath, from the pebbles, in passing, a spark
Struck out by a steed flying fearless and fleet;

The lines following, in which Longfellow describes the sleeping towns of Medford and then Lexington, again evoke new and different things. The excitement is gone, replaced by the somehow sad and yet portentous loneliness of the night. The "crowing of the cock" and the "barking of the farmer's dog" and the feeling of the dampness of the "river fog" all create something quite apart from what has gone before. And then the otherworldly image of the golden weathercock swimming in the moonlight far above, and the disturbing anthropomorphism in the frightening "spectral glare" of the meetinghouse windows like eyes "aghast" at the coming horror of bloodshed.

But at two o'clock, when at last he enters the village of Concord, the mood turns elegiac. The "bleating of the flock" and the "twitter of birds" and the "breath of the morning breeze/Blowing over the meadow brown" all have the sense of something deeply beautiful and sad and imminent. These are the moments in the full darkness before daybreak, when the innocent animals alone sense it, even before the incipient glow of dawn approaches. And then the most powerful and the most heartbreaking image in the poem:

And one was safe and asleep in his bed
Who at the bridge would be first to fall,
Who that day would be lying dead,
Pierced by a British musket ball.

It is a powerfully emotional dilation that Longfellow would now take us aside to gaze for a moment at this man, eighty-five years dead but in the eternal present of this holy moment still young and alive and sleeping, swathed in the innocent protection of slumber and blissfully oblivious to what lies just ahead. We can hardly help imagining that his wife and children are asleep nearby too, also oblivious to the agony of loss they will soon face. Longfellow's point in digressing to show us this sleeping man is to show us that it was men like this—alive and breathing just as we are now alive and breathing and who slept just as we sleep—who rose up at the call of duty and faced whatever might come. It was young men like this who sacrificed themselves for what we now have, for our unfathomable liberties and blessings. Do we appreciate that sacrifice? Longfellow makes it so real that it touches our hearts. He is not an abstract minuteman but a person, asleep.

To see him here as a real, breathing person and not as a historical generalization is what makes this so powerful, because it makes the reader understand that we who are now alive are not any different from him, that we too might be called by events of history to stand dutifully and nobly against injustice and tyranny. It makes us ask ourselves whether, when that call comes, we will stand as he stood. His example and our palpable sense of gratitude for his sacrifice make us want to. All of which culminates in the closing lines, so moving and rousing.

> *For, borne on the night-wind of the Past,*
> *Through all our history, to the last,*
> *In the hour of darkness and peril and need,*
> *The people will waken and listen to hear*
> *The hurrying hoof-beats of that steed,*
> *And the midnight message of Paul Revere.*

So what is Longfellow's poem asking of us who hear it? It is doing what all heroic art does: It asks us to think not merely of ourselves but to think of ourselves as part of something larger—as part of something noble and beautiful and good and true. The men who died at Lexington and in the revolution that followed were not merely dying for themselves and for their families. They were dying for something far beyond that. They were dying for those not yet born. And therefore it is unavoidable: They were dying for us, for you and me. They were dying for the idea in their breasts that men must be free; they were dying for that thing they called liberty. They earnestly believed that what they were dying for was exceptional and noble and true; and they humbly but courageously believed they were in the right, that they were living and fighting not merely for the pinched freedom of their own self-interests but for another kind of freedom, for a higher purpose. They were not cynical. They believed in these things and they fought and died for them. What are we to do about that? Can we forget it? If we remember poems like this one, we will not do so easily.

Longfellow was keenly considering these things in the days just before the violent rupture of the Civil War. Men would be called upon to die for their country—but not merely for their country. Their country stood for something greater than itself, and it was that for which they were being called to make these sacrifices. It was because they were living and dying for others that they could face what lay ahead. We can even see that it was not for America as she was that they died but for the promise of America, for the promise of who she was destined to become. That is the proper role of the heroic, to call us higher than ourselves. To call us to fight not merely for what is ours but for what should belong to everyone—for what is right.

We know that they did, and we must ask whether we will, when our time comes. And we wonder whether our time has come now. When a nation has forgotten who it is at its core, has forgotten not just the important ideas that animated it in the first place but the heroes who brought those ideas to life, are we not facing the same threat faced by Revere's generation and Longfellow's? It matters little whether the challenge is to bring a nation into existence against overwhelming opposition in the last part of the eighteenth century, or to prevent that nation from violently tearing itself asunder in the middle of the nineteenth, or to prevent it from evaporating into nonexistence while no one notices at the beginning of the twenty-first. Longfellow's poem and many other heroic works of art speak to the central issue, which is the same: whether we can keep the republic that has been a beacon of liberty and a promise to the future and to the world.

FIVE

The Importance of Moral Leaders

For everyone to whom much is given, from
him much will be required.

—Jesus of Nazareth

If a self-governing people must possess virtue, and if they encourage virtue by remembering heroic stories and venerating heroes, what about the character of that people's own leaders? How might their character, or lack of it, come into play with regard to our ability to "keep" the fragile republic of ordered freedoms entrusted to us?

There is no doubt that the character of our leaders is important, both in one way we will discuss now and in another far more important way we will discuss at the end of this chapter.

But before we talk about how character in our leaders is important, let's be clear that it is far from the only thing we look for in our leaders. There are other qualities, such as competence and experience and intelligence and an ability to "get the job done," that matter tremendously. And one might possess these in abundance while being less than sterling in the category we are calling "character." A military leader, for example, might be a rogue in his private life, but if he is a brilliant tactician and knows how to win wars, chances are we will find a way to overlook his moral failings. Even here, though, there are limits to what we can overlook, because as was the case quite recently with General Petraeus, leaders involved in extramarital affairs may be blackmailed by foreign powers or may reveal top secret intelligence. Nonetheless we may agree that there are times when sheer competence is what we look for more than anything. Someone piloting a plane, for example, needs to be good at what he does, whatever his moral failings. Few would want to ride in a plane flown by someone not terribly skilled as a pilot, however sterling his character. So character may not be the only criterion worth examining in our leaders. But what role does it play?

Our history is full of leaders whose scores in these various categories in particular would be mixed. Most agree that Nixon was in some ways a great president, a genius of geopolitics and diplomacy, but that he let his insecurity and his ambition to be reelected cloud his judgment and ultimately lead him to make decisions that destroyed him and his larger reputation. Many have said that Jimmy Carter, while a man of solid character, did not have the strength to lead effectively and in the end had a negligible or negative effect on the country. He was said, for example, to be such a micromanager that he actually personally oversaw the scheduling of the White House tennis courts. That he was a Sunday school teacher and devout Christian did not seem to override his administrative and other shortcomings.

In 1997, during the Lewinsky scandal of the Clinton administration, the president's defenders put forth the idea that the head of the executive branch of the U.S. government needed more than anything to be competent, saying that his character was a private issue. The idea was that he was there to do a job, not be a moral role model, and if he was clever and competent and knowledgeable, he could lead well and be a great president. Whether a cynical ploy to divert attention from the behavior of the president or a sincere misunderstanding of how things work in a free society or both, there can hardly be any serious question whether Clinton's moral failings harmed the nation. By refusing to resign his office, as most others at the time would have done if plausibly accused of what he was accused of, he led the country—and by extension the world—through a crisis of leadership at a time when leadership was particularly needed. With the benefit of two decades' retrospect it can plausibly be argued that his actions during the scandal indicate that he valued staying in power and defeating his political opponents more than he valued the country itself. Not only did his choice to fight his accusers drag the culture through a decidedly unpleasant cultural conversation, one for which many parents will never forgive him, but it also devalued the role and dignity of the office of the president. So even if it's true that his moral failings did not initially affect his ability to govern and did not initially affect the country itself, they seem certainly to have done so once he chose to react to his accusers as he did.

Richard Nixon was on both sides of the same equation. Most would agree that his behavior in what led to the Watergate scandal was bad, but that his reaction to the unfolding scandal and his choice to stubbornly fight his detractors was far worse for the country than the initial offenses. Most would also agree that the scandal dramatically hurt the perception of the presidency in general and therefore hurt the country and our ability to govern ourselves effectively, for reasons we will touch upon at the end of this chapter. But what is less known is that twelve years before Watergate, in the wake of an unprecedentedly close election with John F. Kennedy, Nixon might very easily have contested the results—it was widely believed that voter fraud had affected the outcome, perhaps dispositively—but that he did not.

Kennedy's vice-presidential running mate, Lyndon Johnson, was known to be no stranger to dirty politics, and it was indisputable that he threw his considerable political weight around when necessary, and no more so than in seeing to it that whatever unscrupulous advantages could be taken on election night 1960 were taken. Similarly, Democratic Chicago mayor Richard

Daley was an undisputed champion of dirty politics with solid ties to the Chicago mafia, and his push to have votes stolen, especially in Cook County, made a significant difference in Illinois's final tally. But Nixon, when confronted with all of these shenanigans, in the end decided not to press his case. He said that such an action would ultimately harm the country and could lead to a "constitutional crisis"—and he was right. It would have undermined Americans' faith in the electoral process and in their government in general. Whether Nixon was saying this to appear noble or because he actually believed these things—or a combination of both—is ultimately immaterial. He understood that what the American people saw and felt about how the government worked and how their leaders behaved was at the heart of the way our system of government worked. Ironically, it was the shenanigans of the JFK handling of the 1960 election that were said to have pushed Nixon to be less than scrupulous twelve years later. Which gives us one more reason that character matters in our leaders: Whenever one leader behaves unscrupulously, it pushes others to see this either as a new norm, or at least as something encouraging them in the wrong direction. It worked for him; why can't it work for me?

We need leaders who themselves love the country and the freedoms of this country more than they love themselves and their own careers or reputations or "legacies." That is why when a leader is caught doing something ignoble, the most noble thing to do, typically, is to resign, knowing that in the scandal that will be dragged out if they don't, the country will be adversely affected.

And this is the main point to be made here, that the character of our leaders is important because it affects everyone—their peers and those they lead. And if a virtuous people is vital to self-government, as we have established, their virtue cannot help but be affected, in one direction or the other, by the behavior of their leaders. So it follows that leaders—whether political or cultural—may encourage or discourage a wider culture of virtue. And in a nation where a culture of virtue is crucial to the entire system of self-government, character in our leaders is no small thing. We may again recall John Adams's statement that the Constitution cannot contain our untoward passions—that they will break through the Constitution as easily "as a whale goes through a net." So we need a culture of virtue, and our leaders have a vital role to play in that regard.

In talking about heroes we have underscored the idea that there is great power in examples. And it is the most important reason that we remember and venerate heroes, because we learn from their examples and cannot help but wish to emulate them in their heroism. But the larger point is that everyone influences everyone, for good or for ill. And there can be even less question that leaders, whose actions and lives are more known than others', are more influential than others and therefore ought to be held to a higher standard of behavior. All authority figures, whether teachers or coaches or clergymen or doctors or policemen, have a great influence on those they serve. And no one has more of an influence than parents. But the founders placed particular value on the behavior of political leaders and on virtue in general.

When the founders were advocating for liberty, their single-most-quoted source was the Bible, which of course tells us something about their thoughts on the importance of virtue. But the second-most-quoted source was the French political philosopher Montesquieu, who wrote that "bad examples can be worse than crimes." He continued: "More states have perished because of a violation of their mores than because of a violation of their Laws."

What was Montesquieu getting at? It is what we have been discussing, that what our perceived leaders do affects the people they lead. It is simply how human beings are made. We are affected by examples. Every child is affected by the behavior of his parents. No matter what the parents might say with their mouths, it is their example more than anything that speaks to the child about how to behave.

So it's vital that government leaders see that they bear a great responsibility in this regard, that they understand their role in helping create a culture of virtue and a culture of self-government and sacrifice. The founding generation understood this well and often looked back to the Romans for examples of civic virtue. The story of one Roman senator in particular was well known to them and to many generations of Americans, though it is largely forgotten today. This Roman figure was so highly regarded that in 1790 the city called Cincinnati was named after him. Here is his story.

CINCINNATUS AND HIS PLOW

In the Museo Nacional del Prado in Madrid there hangs a famous 1806 painting by Juan Antonio Ribera. It depicts Cincinnatus at his farm, where Roman leaders have just arrived to entreat him to accept the role of Roman dictator. The Roman senate, facing a crisis, has just elected him to serve as dictator for the typical six-month term. (We should be clear that the term "dictator" did not have the negative connotations it does today. It was a carefully prescribed six-month term and was required only in situations of crisis.)

Cincinnatus embodied the Roman ideal of the aristocrat who serves out of duty. He did not wish to leave his farm or to be dictator, but when called upon to serve, he answered. According to the Roman historian Livy, the senators who came to inform him that he had been appointed dictator arrived at his farm to find him out in the fields, plowing. When Cincinnatus heard their message, he immediately called for his toga, which signified the acceptance of his new role. He put on the ceremonial garment at once, at which point all the senators who were there immediately hailed him as dictator—and off to Rome he went.

Cincinnatus's first act as dictator was to call up every able-bodied man to fight. He then heroically led them himself in fighting the Aequi. All of this argues for his nobility; he did his duty for Rome despite preferring not to. At the time of the American Revolution, the founders looked to ancient Greece and Rome as models of what it meant to have a democracy, and therefore when Washington accepted the call of the Continental Congress to lead the Continental Army, he brought to mind Cincinnatus. But it was what Cincinnatus did afterward—and what Washington would do afterward—that made the historical connection between them far more powerful and apt, and made both of them infinitely more noteworthy.

History tells us that Cincinnatus led the Romans to victory quickly and immediately resigned as soon as he had accomplished his mission, a mere fifteen days after he had lifted his hand from the plow. Though elected for six months, he nonetheless voluntarily gave up his unlimited power as dictator and returned to his farm. For this extraordinary act he was instantly and evermore hailed as a hero and model of Roman duty and citizenship. Other than Cincinnatus, no one in history had ever done such a thing. Power was something everyone craved and sought. It was not something anyone gave up voluntarily. But Cincinnatus put the Roman republic before his own ambitions, becoming an unparalleled hero of civic virtue.

At the time of our nation's founding, political leaders on both sides of the Atlantic were influenced by Roman models of civic virtue. William Pitt the Younger in England was well schooled in Roman history and could during a speech or debate instantly produce quotes from Tacitus or other Roman writers. It was part of the culture of the time and without that, it seems impossible that history would have produced this thing we now know of as the United States of America. One notable example from 1783 gives us a striking parallel to the story of Cincinnatus. It is a story every American should know. It is one of the high-water marks of our history and one of the high-water marks of world history. It took place in Newburgh, New York, at the tail end of the War of Independence.

WASHINGTON'S FINEST HOUR

It was noon on March 16, 1783. George Washington's officers were gathered in a building on the Hudson River near Newburgh, New York, where his military headquarters were at the time. The imposing figure, then fifty-one years old, entered the recently constructed lodgelike structure and strode to the podium. He then gave what many consider the most important speech of his life. Many also consider this mostly unknown moment to be the greatest and most heroic moment in a life filled with great and heroic moments.

Before we talk further about this moment, we might first think of other heroic moments. We might think of him standing nobly in the prow of a boat crossing the Delaware River on Christmas night in 1777. (That image is likely fixed in our minds because of the monumental 1851 painting by Emanuel Leutze that today hangs in the Metropolitan Museum in New York City.) We might also think of him at Valley Forge with his troops in the terrible winter of 1777, when so many died, where amid snow and ice his men wrapped their feet in rags for lack of shoes or boots. We might think of him on horseback, bravely leading a charge, as he so often did, taller in the saddle than anyone else and seemingly fearless. History records that he had several horses shot out from under him during the French and Indian War.

There are many moments after the war that we might consider as well. He presided over the Constitutional Convention in 1787, almost in his person holding together the fractured pieces of the fragile federation. If we think of him principally as the first chief executive of the United States, we might picture him in 1789, being inaugurated on the steps of the old Federal Hall near Wall Street in New York City. But arguably it was at that podium that noon in that humble hall overlooking the Hudson that more than anything defines him as great for the ages. The war was just one month from being officially over. The fighting was over, but no one knew that at the time. There were 7,000 troops stationed nearby, lest the British decide to continue fighting.

On April 19, 1783, Washington would order a "cessation of hostilities."

The men and the officers in this room with Washington were all that stood between the British army and the preservation of the independence of the United States of America. It was not yet over, so to speak. And the tension among the officers had grown and grown to an impossible level.

The reason for his speech was a letter that had been anonymously circulated among the officers. Many of them had given years of service to the Continental Army, but after all this time most of them had not yet been paid. Most of them were outraged that Congress had rewarded their service in this fashion. The officers were growing increasingly restless and the letter gave voice to what many had been discussing privately. It proposed that the officers stage a coup and present Congress with a stark ultimatum: Either find the money to pay the officers immediately, or they would walk away from their posts and leave Congress to defend itself against the British—or, more likely, they would themselves seize control of the government. They planned to put their leader, General Washington, at the head of this military dictatorship, because as they saw the situation, he deserved to lead the new country he had fought to create. By way of context, there was nothing unprecedented about this suggestion. Since the beginning of time, military leaders had become heads of state, and when such a leader was someone as noble and brave as the general who had led the colonial troops so self-sacrificially, it was expected he would lead the country. Who better to be the first leader of the independent colonies than the man who had almost single-handedly brought them from tyrannical subjugation to freedom? On the face of it there was nothing at all especially remarkable about what the officers suggested.

But when Washington caught wind of it, he was shocked and furious. His own sense of virtue was such that for him this proposal was offensive. It violated everything he stood for and believed in and for which he had risked his life these eight long years. Because as he understood it, he had been fighting not merely to gain independence from Great Britain but to allow the American colonies to do something that had never been done in the history of the world: govern themselves. There would be no dictatorship or monarchy, benevolent or otherwise. They would be truly free in a way no people had ever been free. This was what he in these years had been fighting for—for a new kind of liberty. And he knew that anything short of that was nothing less than failure. Simply to have another kind of monarchy—and to have even the possibility of another kind of tyranny—was no better than where they had been when the war began at Lexington and Concord in April of 1775. It's quite clear from what he said that he was deeply disappointed that the officers under him didn't understand this.

He began his speech by rebuking them for the "anonymous summons" to gather here, which he deemed "unmilitary" and "subversive of all order and discipline." He then continued:

If my conduct heretofore has not evinced to you that I have been a faithful friend to the army, my declaration of it at this time would be equally unavailing and improper. But as I was among the first who embarked in the cause of our common country. As I have never left your side one moment, but when called from you on public duty. As I have been the constant companion and witness of your distresses, and not among the last to feel and acknowledge your merits. As I have ever considered my own military reputation as inseparably connected with that of the army. As my heart has ever expanded with joy, when I have heard its praises, and my indignation has arisen, when the mouth of detraction has been opened against it, it can scarcely be supposed, at this late stage of the war, that I am indifferent to its interests.

He tells them that despite all they are suffering, he is absolutely convinced Congress is doing all it can to find the money to pay them and will do so.

Why would we distrust them? And why, in consequence of that distrust, adopt measures which will cast a shade over that glory which has been so justly acquired, and tarnish the reputation of an army which has been celebrated throughout all Europe for its fortitude and patriotism?

While I pledge myself in the most unequivocal manner to exert whatever ability I am possessed of in your favour, let me entreat you, gentlemen, on your part, not to take any measures which, viewed in the calm light of reason, will lessen the dignity and sully the glory you have hitherto maintained. . . . Let me conjure you, in the name of our common country, as you value your own sacred honor, as you respect the rights of humanity, and as you regard the military and national character of America, to express your utmost horror and detestation of the man who wishes, under any specious pretenses, to overthrow the liberties of our country, and who wickedly attempts to open floodgates of civil discord and deluge our rising empire in blood.

He went on:

By thus determining and acting . . . you will give one more distinguished proof of unexampled patriotism and patient virtue, rising superior to the pressure of the most complicated sufferings. And you will, by the dignity of your conduct, afford occasion for posterity to say, when speaking of the glorious example you have exhibited to mankind, "Had this day been wanting, the world had never seen the last stage of perfection to which human nature is capable of attaining."

When Washington spoke these final and extraordinary words of his speech, the room fell silent. We can only imagine what was going through the minds of the officers to whom these words had been directed. But what of historical significance would happen that day, at that podium, was not yet over. No one knows whether what Washington did next was planned or spontaneous, but everyone agrees that it served to powerfully affect most everyone in the room and turn the mood dramatically and overwhelmingly toward accepting all he had just said.

Having finished the speech, he told the officers he had something else he wished to read to them, and he reached into his uniform pocket to produce a letter. It was from a Virginia congressman. The handwriting must have been quite small, because after unfolding it and beginning to read it, it was clear Washington was having difficulty in making out what it said. So he reached into his waistcoat pocket and pulled out a pair of wire-rimmed spectacles. He had been using them for some time, but never in view of his officers, so the gesture must have taken them aback. And then came the famous line: "Gentlemen, you must pardon me. I have grown gray in your service and now find myself growing blind."

With these words, the mood of the room changed dramatically. There is no question that many of the angry, battle-hardened officers had been softened and moved by his speech, but now, seeing their noble leader in this unprecedented moment of weakness, they were undone. As Washington read the congressman's letter, many of them actually wept.

There is so much to say about this speech and this moment. Before we discuss the repercussions of it, let's first acknowledge that Washington's language is a far cry from anything we hear today. I am not referring to his lofty and ennobling style of speech, although to some extent that is at issue too. But far more important is his use of specific words and phrases like "reputation," "patient virtue," "dignity," "glory," and "sacred honor."

These words and phrases are most striking to us in that they have disappeared, generally speaking, and not just as words but as concepts. Who speaks of "sacred honor" or "glory" today? These words and ideas have been quietly banished from our cultural conversation. Nor is it that we have replaced these terms with less antiquated equivalents. We've lost them altogether. The question is whether we can ever recover them, and whether, short of that, we can survive. Can it be that the further we have strayed from thinking of such things, the further we have strayed from what is necessary for the ordered liberty bequeathed to us by the founders? And that in neglecting the cultivation of these virtues have we unwittingly undermined our entire way of life?

What we see in Washington here is a man who lives in a world in which virtue and honor are accepted as vital to the life they all wish to lead. There is no possibility that they can get where they wish to go without them. To ignore these things or to mock them would have been unthinkable, and we must wonder how we can have come to a place where that's no longer the case, where to take them seriously is unthinkable for so many, especially in the elite cultural circles of our day.

But all of this is just to say that even in a world where these ideas and standards were at the center of all that mattered, Washington rose far above standard expectations. For one thing, his noble character, evinced so clearly in what he did and how he spoke about it, did what such things always must do. It caused those who heard it to feel what some call "conviction" over their own failures to live and think to that noble standard. They did not reject that standard. They knew it was right and they immediately understood that they had misstepped and must correct themselves.

Washington had voluntarily given up tremendous power, and we may see that this selfless and noble action sums up and points toward the essence of America's promise, of the possibilities and potential of the United States of America. We are most ourselves when we are thinking not of ourselves but of others. If Washington's action made our existence as a republican democracy possible, we see that there are times—and that was one of them—when there is no substitute for virtue. If Washington had in that moment succumbed to the tremendous and understandable pressure to do what was practical and sensible, rather than to do what was so very noble, the United States of America would not exist. We could say that in that historic moment, it was Washington's virtuous character that allowed the United States to be born. How can we as Americans not know and celebrate this man and this example of tremendous character, an example that can be said to have made the entire future of the nation possible? And how can we not believe that such an expression of virtue and selflessness must have gone a tremendously long way in affecting the lives and behavior of the men in the room that day and the life and behavior of every one of his contemporaries who learned of what he had done? Indeed, it would have gone a tremendous way toward encouraging a culture of virtue in those earliest and most important days of our republic.

Washington may well have been influenced by the story of Cincinnatus in doing what he did that day in Newburgh, and there can be no doubt that many have been influenced by the story of Washington, that many of us, remembering this story just told, will be influenced in our own actions. From before Plutarch wrote his *Lives*, human beings have known that heroes inspire us to do what is right when temptation would tempt us otherwise. So in a government like ours, leaders who exemplify virtue do much to help those they lead in self-government. It is obvious that Washington and the other founders were well aware that the public examples they set of virtue were important, that they played a role in creating a culture of virtue that would help the nation govern itself. They knew the limits of the law and of the Constitution they had drafted. The rest was up to the people themselves, who must do their part voluntarily.

But no one better understood these things than a political leader who was not an American but who was a contemporary of Washington's, although they never met; indeed, this great man never set foot on American soil. His influence in creating a culture of virtue in England and beyond is incalculable, and it is worth examining briefly here. His success in this was so great that it arguably enabled him to enact more sweeping social reforms in his country than anyone else in history. So he may be easily reckoned the greatest social reformer in history, and perhaps even the greatest politician too. We are speaking now of William Wilberforce.

"MAKING GOODNESS FASHIONABLE"

If William Wilberforce is known at all, it is principally as the parliamentarian who for two decades championed the cause of the African slaves and in 1807 won victory in abolishing the slave trade throughout the vast British Empire. Abraham Lincoln and Frederick Douglass often lauded him as the great pioneer and first champion of the noble abolitionist cause. And even in his own time, for his seemingly tireless efforts to bring liberty to the African captives Wilberforce was reckoned "the Washington of humanity." The story of that political battle and victory are told in the feature film *Amazing Grace*, which was released in 2007 on the bicentennial of that victory, as they are in my own book of the same title. But it is actually in another capacity, related to that single victory but nonetheless quite different, that his life may have been most influential.

In 1776, when Wilberforce was just seventeen years old and a student at Cambridge University, the British nation was swimming in corruption. John Bull was of course newly embroiled in a war with his upstart cousins across the ocean, and Wilberforce as a young man would sit in the gallery of the House of Lords and watch the great and ultimately historic debates raging on the floor below. Beside him sat his bosom friend and Cambridge classmate William Pitt the Younger, whose father was one of the principals in the debates on the floor below. He led the side against engaging the colonies in war, while Lord North and others took the king's position. As we have already established, it was the king's government that ultimately prevailed in that argument and ultimately lost the war and the colonies. But that is not what concerns us here. What concerns us is the widespread culture of vice that reigned in Great Britain during that era and, even more than that, the decades-long role of William Wilberforce in turning its foul tide.

There was open disregard and even active disdain for public and private morality in Great Britain. In a word, it was fashionable to be immoral, especially among the upper classes. Public drunkenness, even on the very floor of Parliament, was common. The wealthy were typically drunk on claret, while the poor slowly killed themselves with gin, as the famous Hogarth print *Gin Alley* illustrates. Politicians openly traded money for votes; indeed, this was so normal that it was entirely expected. It was a time of open debauchery in every sphere of the culture; such behaviors were flaunted. For one index of the cultural climate, we may recall that during this period in London, 25 percent of all single women were prostitutes; their average age was sixteen.

But as bad as things were throughout the culture, the debauchery flowed—and even gushed—from the top down, a veritable cataract of moral sewage, although to be fair, its fetid source was not the king himself. Though Americans have understandably cast George III as a villain, inasmuch as he was our enemy in the revolution—he can little be faulted in his personal character. He was a devoted father and husband who even read the Bible to his daughters each night. But his sons were another story entirely. His eldest son, the Prince of Wales, who would one day become King George IV, was without peer as a ne'er-do-well and widely known so to be, for example, racking up dizzying mountains of gambling debts that periodically were paid out of the public treasury.

This monarch in waiting—who would also take the title of England's Defender of the Faith—was also widely known for over the careering course of his coarse career to have bedded some seven thousand women. And like some jackalope combination of Casanova and Mengele, to have collected hair samples from each of them and cataloged them in envelopes. The Duke of Wellington once referred to the troubled prince and his dissolute brothers as "the damnedest millstones about the neck of any Government that can be imagined."

So when the foulest figures in the land were the man who would be king and his scrofulous brethren, the tone of the culture suffered much. Profligacy among the wealthy was the fashion of that time, and they fought enthusiastically to outdo one another in gluttonous and bibulous exploits. What's more, they cared nothing for the poor and none of them had the faintest notion that using some of their largesse to help the less fortunate might be advisable. It was simply not an idea that occurred to them, nor were the lukewarm preachers in their Church of England pulpits in the habit of rocking anyone's bejeweled boats.

Wilberforce was in his college years and in his first years as a young parliamentarian part of that profligate scene. Like his friends and colleagues, he would eat and drink and sing and gamble into the wee hours of many mornings and was at one time a member of five London gentlemen's clubs where most of these activities were the only ones from which to choose. But in 1785, during a round-trip carriage ride of some thousands of miles to the French and Italian rivieras with a certain polymath genius named Isaac Milner, Wilberforce found religion, and upon his return he gave up his previous activities and in two

years' time famously chose to devote himself to abolishing the
slave trade in Parliament. But what is less known is that he simultaneously took on a host of social evils, ones that did not
affect the African slaves but that did mostly affect the poor of
his own nation, and he ultimately succeeded in defeating many
of them and in dramatically changing the cultural climate. And
what must be said for our purposes here is that he knew that it
was not only in his position as a legislator and parliamentarian
that he could effect change. He saw that the larger culture of
vice made it impossible to do anything legislatively, and that if
he wished to help those who were suffering he must undertake
a campaign to change the whole cultural climate. He understood that culture flowed from the top down and that culture
was upstream of politics. So unless he could make inroads
there—somehow—he would never succeed in passing any bills
toward these ends.

He famously said that he hoped to "make goodness fashionable," but he was under no illusions that this would be either
easy to do or even possible. But he wondered whether he might
do something in this direction and make his colleagues in Parliament—and in other precincts of power—see that their behavior and the laws of the land were in fact causing tremendous
harm not just to the poor but to the nation at large. He wondered whether it might be possible to get some members of high
society to strive to outdo one another in good works and charity, as much as they had once striven to outdo one another in

lavish parties and gluttony and drunkenness. It would be the steepest of uphill climbs, but Wilberforce had youth on his side, and in the course of four decades we can conclude that against all odds—and every ugly devil of hell—he succeeded.

Wilberforce understood the idea that the law itself is a "teacher" and will lead people toward what it prescribes and away from what it prohibits. But he knew that a debased culture cannot be stemmed through legislation alone. Indeed, if one wishes to make certain laws, one must change the culture first, else those laws will never be passed.

In the case of the slave trade, Wilberforce knew that what he wished to do would culminate in a law and that he would need to introduce a bill into Parliament and lobby for its passage. But for this political effort to succeed, he must first convince the members of Parliament—and the millions of Britons who would vote for them—that the slave trade was morally wrong. He must work outside the law, and within the culture, to change the law. In other words, unless he could create enough of a culture of virtue for people and their parliamentary representatives to want to vote against their immediate best interests and for the best interests of people they would never meet and the long-term interests of the nation at large, the glimmerings of democracy in Britain would be worthless. Even he saw that without a moral populace, the nation's laws could do little; and he saw that without a leadership class that made some effort toward at least the appearance of virtue, those who voted would be led astray.

He understood that certain cultural leaders set the tone and "set the fashion in terms of moral norms—which are the mores" and "habits of the heart" of which Tocqueville would write several decades later. Wilberforce also knew that he was one of these cultural leaders and that he could influence not only those beneath him in society but also his peers, for even greater effect. For one thing, Wilberforce was openly and vocally religious at a time when most cultural leaders scorned religion, thinking it a relic of the unenlightened past. But Wilberforce's great wit and intelligence, coupled with his good cheer and his willingness to work on vital causes with many who were decidedly irreligious, over time persuaded many in his direction. He became known not as a pious moralist but as someone who seemed to really express love toward the political enemies who were everywhere around him, especially on the bitter issue of the slave trade.

Another thing that Wilberforce did that was a dramatic departure from the cultural norm in his social sphere was spend a great deal of time with his children. He and his wife had six of them, and Wilberforce was known to spend every Sunday with them almost exclusively, wrestling on the lawn with his boys, giving them piggyback rides and generally doing what a good father does who loves his children. But in the milieu of that time and place, prominent leaders simply did not spend time with their families. They did what men do and left the domestic sphere to their wives. Wilberforce markedly changed that and many other fashions over time.

Wilberforce's great effort to "making goodness fashionable" succeeded so dramatically over a number of decades that it became popular for wealthy people—women especially—to form small groups dedicated to this or that charitable cause. At one point Wilberforce himself was listed in the leadership or membership of sixty-nine of them. These were causes ranging from changing the horrendous child labor laws of the time to abolishing public exhibits of animal cruelty to prison reforms to supporting indigent women and children, and many other things. And there is no doubt that the idea of forming such groups leaped across the Atlantic and caught on in America too, first in Lyman Beecher's church in Brooklyn Heights and then around the country. Because of Wilberforce's character and leadership in helping other leaders attend to their characters, "doing good" and "helping the poor" and other causes are generally accepted as important for any leader or celebrity who wishes to be thought well of. If a celebrity or politician were today to say, "I don't care about the poor. Let them care about themselves," they would rightly be shunned and ostracized. But before Wilberforce dragged these ideas into the mainstream of Western culture, this was simply not the case.

Wilberforce's efforts illustrate that the character and behavior of political leaders in a culture can be incalculable. His own efforts were ultimately so successful that the Victorian era that followed Wilberforce was especially known for the opposite of the era that preceded it, for being a culture with a public sense of morality so pronounced that in the years since we have even ridiculed it as an era obsessed with that subject. But for our purposes what is most important in this issue of the character of a nation's leaders is not merely that the virtuous behavior of leaders encourages a culture of virtue in general—however terribly important that is—which in turn enables the people to govern themselves more effectively. What is more important still is that if at any point in a republic of self-government the people begin to distrust their leaders as somehow corrupt or as more concerned with themselves than with those they serve, the whole skein of self-government begins to unravel and is fatally threatened.

SELF-GOVERNMENT CANNOT EXIST WITHOUT VIRTUOUS LEADERS

In a republic such as the one bequeathed to us by the founders, bad examples among our leaders do something even worse than encourage a culture of vice in those they lead; they actually undermine the people's faith in the larger order. So any perceived lack of virtue on the part of our leaders plays a decisive role in undermining the entire enterprise of self-government.

This is because to the people who vote, their elected leaders are inevitably representatives of the larger order of things. In order for self-government to work, citizens must believe that the larger order to which they are giving themselves is essentially trustworthy and solid. They must believe that it's real, that the system works and that their efforts toward self-government matter. They must believe that they really are governing themselves through the leaders they have elected. Once they think the system is corrupt, or that their leaders and representatives are corrupt, it's nearly impossible for the citizens to feel they are anymore part of an actual system of self-government. They will feel less good about paying their taxes, for fear that their money is being misused. It will also be difficult for them to want to give of themselves in military service, for fear that such service and sacrifice aren't worth the trouble. They will generally become cynical about the whole operation and will slowly pull back and make the end of self-government inevitable.

Corruption in leaders gives citizens the sense that they are, in fact, not all in it together. They will get the positively fatal idea that there is indeed an "us" and a "them." At this point the unavoidably central idea that "we the people" are governing ourselves is doomed. The citizens will buy into the deeply pernicious idea that rather than ruling themselves, they are in fact being ruled by others—that all the talk of self-government and liberty is a sham. So they won't work with the government, but will see themselves as dupes of the government and will begin working against it, whether actively or passively. They may be more inclined to cheat on their taxes, or in being less involved in government service, or they may simply stop voting, because they have the idea that the whole thing is somehow rigged against them, so that their vote doesn't matter, and that voting is for suckers. Or they may themselves become actively cynical and vote, but not for the best and noblest candidate, but for the candidate who will put the most money in their pockets—for the one who will get them what they want at the expense of the larger enterprise. They will care for themselves more than for the welfare of the country, because they have ceased to take pride in the country or to see it as a real extension of themselves—as indeed "their" country. So democracy without real patriotism moves toward the destruction of the ordered liberty bequeathed to us by the founders. At that point self-government is doomed, and we are no longer "keeping" the republic but are letting it go to seed.

One of the most fragile parts of our fragile system of ordered liberties is the necessity of a basic trust between the people and their leaders. The republican form of government, with citizens electing representatives, is set up in part as a check and a balance against the mob rule that pure democracy can be. But the people must believe that these leaders are indeed their leaders and their representatives, that these politicians will have the best interests of those who elected them, and the best interests of the whole country, at heart. They must also believe that they are electing leaders who will balance the "pure" self-interest that begins to look like corruption with an understanding of what is right for the greater good beyond their district. It is easy to get this balance wrong in either direction.

For example, some leaders are so obsessed with proving themselves to their constituents that they fight hard in Congress for what we have come to call "legislative pork," which is to say expensive projects that have everything to do with bringing money and jobs into their own district but which do not properly take into consideration whether these things are good for the nation overall. This comes close to corruption, but it is legal, so it cannot actually be called corruption. Nonetheless it undermines the trust of the entire nation in legislators and in the whole system of representative government when it is believed that some legislators are doing this. As a result, two things can happen, and both are bad. Either people will demand that their own legislators do the same, making it an all-out brawl for federal monies, in which everyone loses, because the federal budget will go higher and higher, much like the arms race between the Soviets and the United States, where the idea is that "the other guy is doing it, so we have no choice but to follow suit." Or citizens may check out of the system altogether, denouncing it as corrupt and not only refusing to compete in such a dirty system but also refusing to care much or participate in the democratic process at all. They effectively remove themselves, figuring that to vote is to waste one's time.

But elected representatives can also get this balance wrong in the other way. Sometimes, rather than overdo currying favor with their constituents, some elected leaders effectively abandon them, often by caring about themselves and their careers more than about the people they serve. Self-interest in this case may drive them to curry favor with the press so that their national profile increases, often so that they can seek higher office. For these people the whole game is less about serving those who have elected them than about using their position and their constituents as a stepping-stone to higher office.

This is why Washington and Wilberforce are such role models for politicians. Both of them set the bar so high that it encouraged others to do so and thereby encouraged trust in those who had elected them. Washington understood that what he did, not just in the incident mentioned above but in many others—and how his actions came across to those he led and to those who would elect him—had profound importance because of their immeasurable reach into the future health of the republic. So each leader who is elected in our time must measure himself against that standard, knowing that the trust of the American people in their government—as truly being their government and as indeed being a government of "we the people"— is nothing less than the very life of the government. So even the idea, sometimes mentioned in our elections, that the people of America need to "take back our government" is a shocking indictment of how far we have moved, not merely from where we should be but from where we absolutely must be if we are to survive.

SIX

"*The Almost Chosen People*"

*The position of the Americans is therefore
quite exceptional, and it may be believed
that no democratic people will ever be
placed in a similar one.*

—Alexis de Tocqueville, *Democracy in
America* (1835)

To some extent this is a book about what's been
called "American exceptionalism," which is rightly
and wrongly something of a controversial subject. It is only controversial because it's most often been tragically misunderstood.
Yet understanding it correctly is foundationally crucial to
"keeping" the republic bequeathed to us by the founders in 1787.

What exactly is American "exceptionalism" and where did that idea come from? Alexis de Tocqueville, whom we have mentioned, is credited with coining the word "exceptional" as related to this concept in this passage from his landmark work *Democracy in America*: "The position of the Americans is therefore quite exceptional, and it may be believed that no democratic people will ever be placed in a similar one." That it was not an American but a Frenchman who first put forward that word and to some extent the concept of American exceptionalism makes the larger and important point that the source of American exceptionalism should have nothing to do with excesses of nationalistic chest-beating and jingoistic hubris. We may take some real comfort in knowing that its first appearance was in a foreigner's cold-eyed analysis and subsequent wonderment at this country, when she was young.

Although the term as applied to America began with Tocqueville, the idea that there was something "exceptional"—or singular—about America, that America had a particular destiny or telos began over two centuries before Tocqueville, before America became a nation. Indeed that idea is inextricably intertwined with America. This is because America was an idea even before the founders gave us a nation based on that idea. It was a hope and a promise more than 150 years before that hope and that promise took the form of a government and a nation. The question is whether more than two centuries after the idea became a nation the idea can continue to live, or whether the nation has eclipsed the idea and effectively killed it.

For such a thing to happen is typical of ideas in history. Once they become settled or codified into institutions, the temptation is to look to the institution that was created by the idea and eventually to forget the idea and mistake the institution for the idea. This temptation and challenge happened to the Christian church in the fourth century when the Roman emperor Constantine made Christianity the "official" religion of the Roman Empire. It went from being a persecuted minority to being an institution, protected by the government. So the temptation arose to blur the two. Rather than looking to God, one might look to the structure of the official institution—or even to the authority of the government that supported it. We must forever refresh ourselves and reclaim our roots, or what was once fresh and green will harden and ossify and die. Those of us who call ourselves Americans have that choice before us today. We can be citizens of a nation that is not America but "America"—or by being Americans and fulfilling our duties as such we can prune the thorny punctuation choking her and free her to truly live and breathe.

It's important that we examine the principal idea of America, the idea that existed before the nation, that gave birth to the nation. But let's first look at why America is often said to be exceptional.

The great writer G. K. Chesterton once said that "America is the only nation that is founded on a creed." We have touched upon this in a previous chapter, but it is worth underscoring. How can it be that with roughly two hundred countries in the world today, America is still the only one that can be described that way? And yet it is. And the creed upon which it is founded is not a parochial creed but a universal one, declaring that all men are created equal and that government exists only by the consent of the governed. As President Truman put it, "Being an American is more than a matter of where you or your parents came from. It is a belief that all men are created free and equal." This touches upon another way we are exceptional. We do not give preference based on one's family or one's race or beliefs. We are a merit-based society where people of every background can rise as they please. Of course, there are caveats to this idea, but the truth is nonetheless overwhelming. We are a nation with so many rags-to-riches stories that we hardly bother to tell them anymore. We are ourselves a rags-to-riches story, and the stories of many of our leaders, from Abraham Lincoln to Thomas Edison to Oprah Winfrey, bespeak this as a central part of our national identity.

America is exceptional too, in that in the more than two centuries since its founding it has continued as a free nation, and not just continued but thrived, and our freedoms have expanded, going a long way toward fulfilling our initial promise. The uniquely ordered freedoms given to us by the founders have produced a nation of extraordinary wealth. With less than 5 percent of the world's population, the United States nonetheless produces more than 25 percent of the world's goods and services. And it is exceptional, finally, in that it values the individual over the state, and that all are subject to the impartial rule of law. In this sense every American is truly of equal value to the most powerful American. We hold our leaders accountable to the same laws every American must follow. If one wishes to point out that this does not always work perfectly, it is not because we don't take it seriously. Indeed, whenever we see the wealthy or the elite favored over those beneath them, there is a public outcry and an attempt to fix the loophole that has allowed it. One need only think of the calls for the impeachment of President Richard Nixon to see that no one in America is above the law, nor should be. Congressmen, senators, and governors have all gone to jail.

But while all of these things may be listed to explain why America is exceptional, they don't really get to the heart of the matter. Again, we may turn to the founders and Tocqueville for the answer to this question. It was the virtuous behavior of Americans, driven principally by their thriving faith in the God of the Bible. It was this far more than anything else. Without that we would be like a body with everything but the heart. This was the animating principle and force behind everything else.

But then we have to ask, what does it really mean to be good? We have to conclude that for the founders and for many before and since, being "good" means believing there is a God who expects us to do unto others as we would have others do unto us, both locally and globally. It means that unlike every other democratic republic in existence, faith in the God of Abraham, Isaac, and Jacob still continues to play a major role in our public life, and that that faith and the outgrowth of that faith is somehow at the core of our success—and that this began long before our founding.

THE SHINING CITY ON A HILL

We may trace the seed of what we think of as American exceptionalism back to the summer of 1630, when a fleet of eleven ships sailed from England to what is today Boston. The fleet's flagship was the *Arbella* and on board her was the man chosen to be governor of the new Massachusetts Bay Colony, John Winthrop. It was probably while aboard that ship during that historic crossing that he delivered his now famous sermon, "A Model of Christian Charity."

In that sermon he said that the future settlement of these people headed to the New World would be a "city upon a hill." It was a significant statement, not meant to be taken lightly, and his hearers, all steeped in the Christian scriptures, would have understood the reference immediately. Winthrop was referring to Jesus's statement from the Gospel of Matthew: "You are the light of the world. A city that is set on a hill cannot be hid."

When Jesus said it he was speaking to his followers in general and for all time, but now Winthrop was applying it to these followers of Jesus about to inaugurate a new kind of settlement in a new world. He was making clear to them that what they were about to do was a tremendous burden, that they bore a responsibility to all other peoples then living and to history—and to the future. "[W]e must consider that we shall be as a city upon a hill," he said,

> *The eyes of all people are upon us. So that if we shall deal falsely with our God in this work we have under-taken, and so cause Him to withdraw His present help from us, we shall be made a story and a by-word through the world.*

So in case anyone sailing from England to the New World had forgotten, he proclaimed that what they were doing was not merely running from religious persecution, which was considerable in the country they had called home until that summer. It was true that they wanted to live their lives in a place where they had the freedom to practice their religion, but this trip was not merely about finding a place where they might live their lives in peace. For them, living their lives in peace meant they would have the opportunity to fulfill their responsibility to do something important for God. They understood that freedom was not merely the freedom to be left alone; it was the freedom to do what was right. Freedom was a gift from God and they must use it for his purposes, and that was their intention. They did not have an abbreviated idea of freedom, as though it were merely freedom from being bothered by others, but rather they saw it as a gift specifically to be used *for* others. Winthrop was reminding them that God would hold them responsible for how they behaved, because of those who would be watching—for the sake of those people, whoever they were, beyond their community.

This idea of freedom as something to be used in the service of others is at the very heart of the Jewish and Christian Scriptures; and through Winthrop and the Puritans of Massachusetts it became an important idea at the heart of the American project in the seventeenth century and in the centuries after. The first place in the Hebrew Scriptures where this idea is mentioned is in the very beginning of the Old Testament. In Genesis chapter 12, God speaks to Abraham about how he will use him to bring the nation of Israel into being, but he makes clear to Abraham that the point of it is that Israel will bless others beyond itself. It is less about Israel than about the God who chose Israel to be his vessel to reach the rest of the world. That is the great blessing and the terrible burden of being chosen by God.

So far from being a selfish idea, it is the idea of living for *others*—of showing them a new way of living—that was at the heart of America. To miss that is to miss everything. This idea of being as a "city upon a hill" that can be seen from afar—and that will be seen from afar—has been with us from the beginning. It is the idea that what we have is indeed something extraordinary, but because of this we have been given the tremendous burden of stewarding and sharing what we have with the rest of the world. So if we are exceptional, we are not exceptional for our own sakes. We are exceptional for the world beyond our shores, for all who are interested in seeing what we are doing and in joining our project.

Seen properly, this is a great burden. But it is one that we have taken quite seriously all these centuries, however imperfectly. It has been a clear and striking part of our national identity. One of the most obvious ways in which we have done this is in welcoming others to our shores. Emma Lazarus's famous poem "The New Colossus," now emblazoned on the base of the Statue of Liberty, is a powerful expression of that aspect of our national identity, and her poem has transformed the meaning of the statue itself to principally reflect this. In the poem Lazarus exclaims a distinctly American *cri de coeur*. She seems in the poem to say what Winthrop was saying nearly three centuries earlier, that the glory of our existence is that we exist for others. It is at the heart of who we are and hope forever to be. The poem refers in its title and first two lines to the Colossus of Rhodes, one of the lost ancient wonders of the world, which stood athwart the harbor of that city and whose meaning to those who saw it was vastly different from that of this noble woman, welcoming struggling immigrants.

Not like the brazen giant of Greek fame,
With conquering limbs astride from land to land;
Here at our sea-washed, sunset gates shall stand
A mighty woman with a torch, whose flame
Is the imprisoned lightning, and her name
Mother of Exiles. From her beacon-hand
Glows world-wide welcome; her mild eyes command
The air-bridged harbor that twin cities frame.[1]

"Keep, ancient lands, your storied pomp!" cries she
With silent lips. "Give me your tired, your poor,
Your huddled masses yearning to breathe free,
The wretched refuse of your teeming shore.
Send these, the homeless, tempest-tost to me,
I lift my lamp beside the golden door!"

Of course, this idea of welcoming others doesn't necessarily mean we can accommodate whoever would like to come, but it means that we very much want to accommodate them and that we will accommodate them as far as conceivably possible. This is at the heart of American identity. In all of the controversies surrounding the subject of immigration, both sides acknowledge we are a nation of immigrants. Many who speak most strongly against immigration today do so because they believe we become less able to accommodate immigrants in the long run if we do not create a fair way of accommodating them in the short run. Very few are foolish enough to say that we don't want immigrants at all. They are widely considered to be our strength. The only real questions are in the details, though for all of the smoke and fury on the issue, few would know that.

Second, living for others means that we want to show the rest of the world that we care, and whenever possible the United States has been first in line to help with tragedies around the world. It is a simple fact that when it comes to spending money and sending medicine and other supplies, not to mention aid workers, we have been by a wide margin the most generous nation in the world. This is perhaps the most distinctly Christian aspect of how we have exemplified this aspect of our national character.

Third, it means that at times we have even gone to war around the globe, knowing that we play a central role not just in things that are a direct threat, but also in fighting anything and anyone who is a threat to democracy and freedom around the world. The details of this may be argued, of course, but what cannot be argued is that we have at times heeded the call of others for military help, the most notable instance of which was that of Winston Churchill and the English people, who knew that without their English-speaking cousins across the Atlantic, they eventually would have fallen to the Nazi forces.

Fourth, we have tried to export our ideas about freedom around the world, with varying success. We have never felt these things were meant for us alone, but rather that they are ideas that are genuinely true and good and intended for anyone who would have them. The tremendous economic success of India and the sea change in China are examples from recent decades, but our ideas about freedom—freedom of the press and freedom of religion—have generally spread throughout the West. We have sometimes been overzealous and intellectually sloppy in promoting these things, and our efforts have sometimes backfired, but that's another story for another time. The point is that except for rare isolationist episodes in our history, we have wanted not to keep these ideas for ourselves but to share them with the world, and in the main this has been a force for good, for us and the world both.

These ideas have been with us from before the founders into the present, and they have been carried forward by Republicans and Democrats from the beginning of our republic into the present—as has that specific phrase "shining city on a hill." Many of us remember President Reagan's repeated use of it in the 1980s, but it was prominently mentioned two decades earlier by President-elect John Kennedy in a speech he gave to the Massachusetts General Assembly days before his inauguration:

I have been guided by the standard John Winthrop set before his shipmates on the flagship Arbella *three hundred and thirty-one years ago, as they, too, faced the task of building a new government on a perilous frontier. "We*

*must always consider," he said, "that we shall be as a city
upon a hill—the eyes of all people are upon us."*

Lest anyone miss the central idea, Kennedy concluded with
the words of Jesus from the Gospel of Luke: "Of them to whom
much is given, much will be required." This is the distinctly
Christian idea that Winthrop meant by referencing Jesus's
"shining city on a hill": that we are inescapably exceptional and
therefore inescapably burdened with the responsibility to help
others. We are not like others, and we may not judge ourselves
as though we were like others. We have a special mission and a
calling to be an example to the world, and to do what we can
with our gifts to help others. Reading Kennedy, we understand
that we cannot dismiss this as a conservative idea resurrected
by Reagan.

Nonetheless in the popular consciousness it is Reagan who
is thought responsible for bringing these words and this idea
into the contemporary conversation. He used the phrase in his
1984 acceptance speech at the Republican convention and again
in his final words to the nation in early 1989. On January 11,
from the Oval Office, he said:

*I've spoken of the shining city all my political life, but I
don't know if I ever quite communicated what I saw when
I said it. But in my mind it was a tall proud city built on
rocks stronger than oceans, wind-swept, God-blessed, and*

teeming with people of all kinds living in harmony and peace, a city with free ports that hummed with commerce and creativity, and if there had to be city walls, the walls had doors and the doors were open to anyone with the will and the heart to get here. That's how I saw it and see it still.

Reading Reagan, we see that this most conservative of modern presidents, even in underscoring this idea of American exceptionalism, pointedly expressed the idea that America existed for others, for those not yet here among us.

So if this is an idea that has been at the very core of our identity from before the beginning, can we truly continue to be America if we forget it?

Finally, when talking of the exceptionalism that has been acknowledged all through our history, when talking of the burden that comes with it, we come to another concept that is even beyond exceptionalism, that of being chosen by God.

Although we will see toward the end of this chapter that it was Abraham Lincoln who coined the phrase God's "almost chosen people" to describe America, and that he sincerely felt that we were called to fulfill "an uncommon promise" to the whole world, he was only one in a long line of many of our greatest leaders who saw things similarly. So before we come to Mr. Lincoln, let's review two earlier episodes from our history that underscore this idea that he expressed.

THE MIRACLE OF SQUANTO

The first of these two episodes goes back a decade before John Winthrop on the *Arbella* to the Pilgrims on the *Mayflower* and a story concerning their first months that, while astonishing, is little known. It concerns an Indian named Squanto. Most Americans have heard of Squanto, but usually just as someone who helped the Pilgrims plant corn using a fish for fertilizer. But few of us know the whole story, which beggars belief, though all of the historical documents exist to corroborate it. Some details are in dispute, but the main points are not, and they are what concern us here.

Most of us, of course, know the Pilgrims landed at Plymouth Rock in 1620, but few of us realize numerous other white Europeans had earlier come to that part of North America to trade with the natives. They hadn't settled there, so we don't remember them. This story begins in approximately 1608, when an English ship with a Captain Hunt sailed south along the coast of what is now called Cape Cod. Finally, Hunt's ship set anchor off the coast of what is today Plymouth, Massachusetts. The Native American tribe on that coast was called the Patuxets, and a number of braves greeted the sailors who rowed ashore. One of the youngest was a boy of about twelve, named Tisquantum, or Squanto.

But this time the Englishmen had darker intentions than trading, brutally capturing some of the braves and taking them to the ship. They then sailed to Málaga, Spain, and sold them as slaves. Somehow Squanto was bought—or rescued, we're not sure—by a group of friars, who evidently treated him well and familiarized him with the Christian religion. They even arranged for him to travel to London around 1612, with the wild idea that he might there find a ship that could take him home again. The idea of expecting to get back to his village in the New World is itself nearly incomprehensible. But Squanto made his way to the London of Shakespeare and James I and found work in the stable of a man named Slaney, where he learned the ways of the English and their language.

And as hoped, a ship was found in 1618 that agreed to take him back to the New World, in exchange for his service as an interpreter. The ship crossed the ocean, with an extended stay in Newfoundland, and then made its way south along the shore of what is today Maine and Massachusetts, where Squanto was released, not far from the place he had been kidnapped a decade before. As he had long dreamed, he managed to make his way back to the very spot where he had grown up. But to his great confusion and disappointment, there was no one there to greet him. What had happened? It is hard to fathom what he must have felt, having dreamed of this day for ten years, only to have his hopes dashed in this most horrible way.

As far as we know, nearly every member of the Patuxet tribe was killed by diseases inadvertently brought by the various traders. Had Squanto been there at the time, he would surely have perished with the rest of his people. But at the time, we may assume, he didn't feel lucky to have been spared alone. At first he wandered to another nearby tribe, but for Squanto the nearby tribes were as much foreigners as the Spanish or English would have been. In fact, after five years among the English, it's possible they seemed less foreign to him than these native people who were not his own Patuxets. So it seems that eventually he decided to live alone in the woods.

But what happened next is the strangest part of the whole story. At about this same time, a group of people we have already mentioned were on board a small ship called the *Mayflower*. They had been in Holland for a number of years to escape the religious persecution in England. It's little mentioned how viciously this group of sincere Christians was persecuted for not adhering to the British Crown's idea of Christian faith. The Plymouth Colony governor William Bradford described the conditions that had driven them to Holland:

> *But after these things they could not long continue in any peaceable condition, but were hunted & persecuted on every side, so as their former afflictions were but as flea-bitings in comparison of these which now came upon them. For some were taken & clapt up in prison, others had their houses beset & watched night and day & hardly escaped their hands; and yet most were faine to flee & leave their houses & habitations, and the means of their livelihood.*

But living in Holland brought other difficulties, so in the end they decided it would be better to strike out into the great unknown, to sail across the Atlantic, hoping to start anew and found a colony that was openly based on Christian principles, where they could live in peace and bring God's light to a new continent. William Bradford recounted that decision in his journal too, in the passage from which we get the word "Pilgrims" to describe these brave men and women.

> *So they lefte [that] goodly & pleasante citie, which had been their resting place, near 12 years; but they knew they were pilgrimes, & looked not much on these things; but lift up their eyes to the heavens, their dearest [country], and quieted their spirits.*

Their journey was itself a great trial. There was a second boat, the *Speedwell*, which did not make it beyond the coast of England, so everyone had to be transferred to the *Mayflower*. There were 102 in all who would make the journey, including about 30 crew. They left in the first week of September 1620, and because the ship was ill suited to the westerly Atlantic winds, it took them two months to make the journey. During the trip two people died, one crew member and one passenger. A baby was born too, whom they named Oceanus.

About halfway across the Atlantic a number of storms struck and a main beam cracked. The damage was so bad that they considered turning back, but in the end they repaired it and were able to continue. But their celebrated landing on the bleak, frigid shores of what is today Cape Cod caused a number of them to sleep in miserably cold and wet conditions. Many of them became ill, and within months half of them had died. In their agony they prayed to God to show them the way forward, but they suspected that returning to England was their most prudent course. But then something unexpected took place.

One day in the spring of 1621 a local native walked out of the woods to greet them. Somehow he actually spoke perfect English; and as it happened, he had grown up on the very land where they had settled. Because of this, he knew everything there was to know about how to survive there. He knew and showed them the best way to plant corn and squash so that they would thrive in that environment. He knew and showed them how to find fish and lobsters and eels there. He knew and showed them much that they couldn't have known themselves. And because his tribe had perished, he had little better to do than help these suffering strangers.

So the Pilgrims adopted him. And Squanto helped them immeasurably, likely saving their lives and almost certainly making it possible for them to continue there on this foreign soil. Could this all have been happenstance?

The Pilgrims didn't think so. To them it seemed nothing less than a miracle of God. In fact, Bradford wrote in his journal that

Squanto "became a special instrument sent of God for [our] good . . . [who] never left [us] till he died."

Squanto also helped the Pilgrims establish a peace with the local Native Americans that lasted fifty years, a stunning accomplishment considering the troubles that settlers would have with native tribes in the centuries following. Sadly, Squanto died not long after this, but Bradford wrote that Squanto "desir[ed] the Governor to pray for him, that he might go to the Englishmen's God in heaven." Squanto even bequeathed his possessions to the Pilgrims "as remembrances of his love."

That this happened is a matter of historical record. That many would interpret it as indicating God's hand on that fledgling colony and the nation that would eventually grow out of it is hardly surprising, especially given that that's how Bradford and the others interpreted it. We also now know that if Bradford and the Pilgrims had returned to England in defeat, Winthrop and the *Arbella* never would have set sail and established the much larger Massachusetts Bay Colony, with its noble ideal of a people who were a "shining city on a hill." So Squanto's long and strange and painful journey had a purpose far beyond anything even he or the Pilgrims realized.

THE MIRACLE OF THE U.S. CONSTITUTION

A second episode that gave many of our founders the idea that they were being guided by an unseen hand was the drafting of the Constitution, to which I referred in my opening pages. It's virtually impossible for us to fully appreciate today what we have in that document. It's lasted for two and a third centuries and has enabled us to have what is simply the most free and prosperous nation in the history of the world. To all who have studied it in these many generations, it is a work of political genius. But to many of the principal players who were there in Independence Hall during those one hundred days of its creation, it seemed the result of something like a miracle too. The men who described it that way were hardly theological zealots.

Its birth required more of those putting it together than we can fairly expect. After all, the men assembled there were politicians, each representing his own state's interests. The sacrifices each was asked to make for the whole were more than seemed reasonable and right. But somehow—and one must underscore that somehow—they did, and the remarkable document that we call the Constitution was drafted and accepted.

But the number of disagreements during the hundred days of the Constitutional Convention boggles the mind. Those who had been there for the revolution and who had despised the tyranny of the British government were tremendously suspicious of doing anything that would strengthen the federal government. So they wanted the states to function like little countries. But as we know, this had not been working. The wiser persons of that era knew that something more needed to be done, else the noble experiment that was the United States of America could not last much longer. The trick was to strengthen the federal government just enough, but not too much. And the question was simply whether this was possible. Wasn't it entirely possible that what they were trying to do could not be done? Wasn't it possible that because it had never been done before it was impossible, that history had proved that and would prove it forever?

And these were not merely disagreements that arose out of selfishness and parochial political viewpoints. In fact, most of the disagreements arose out of the principles held by these men. For example, James Madison strongly advocated that both sides of Congress—the Senate and the House—should have numbers of representatives based on the states' populations. We know that he lost that battle—and that in the end the Senate has two members from each state, whether from a state with a huge population like New York or California, or from a state with a tiny population, like Alaska or Delaware. We also know that Alexander Hamilton believed the president and senators should be chosen for life, just as Supreme Court justices are appointed for life. On and on these various disagreements and arguments raged, without the sense that they eventually would be resolved.

Among the most contentious of these issues was that of slavery, and specifically how much toward a state's population a slave should count. The compromise that listed every American-owned slave as three fifths of a free person is often cited to argue that the Constitution says that slaves are inherently less valuable than free men and women, but this is simply untrue and distorts things grotesquely. It was in fact the northern, antislavery states that wanted to put this in the document. That's because the "slave states" selfishly and cynically wanted their powerless slaves to count toward their states' official populations—so that these states would have more power in Congress. Because the number of representatives in the House of Representatives goes by a state's population, counting slaves would give much more power to the slave states. If slaves were counted, those who owned them would get more power, and of course, the slaves would get none. The northern free states knew that that was wrong. But in order to move ahead, they were forced to compromise, eventually deciding that the slavery states could count their slave populations as three fifths of what they had wanted. So quite contrary to what is often understood, the three-fifths clause was a hard-fought victory for the free states over the slave states. Like many compromises, it had its ugly side. But like many compromises, it worked, and in this case it made possible a nation that would one day abolish slavery altogether and forever.

But toward the end of the convention, after endless battles and little progress, things looked hopeless. The disagreements and arguments had mounted to an impossible height, so the eldest delegate, Benjamin Franklin, gave a speech to the assembly, imploring them to turn to God to break the impasse. Franklin and Jefferson were the least overtly religious of the founders, so the idea that Franklin should be the one to beseech the assembly to turn to God in prayer for an answer to their problems is evidence of their desperation, and it is startling. Here is his remarkable speech:

Mr. President

The small progress we have made after four or five weeks close attendance & continual reasonings with each other, our different sentiments on almost every question, several of the last producing as many noes and ayes, is methinks a melancholy proof of the imperfection of the Human Understanding. We indeed seem to feel our own want of political wisdom, since we have been running about in search of it. We have gone back to ancient history for models of Government, and examined the different forms of those Republics which having been formed with the seeds of their own dissolution now no longer exist. And we have viewed Modern States all round Europe, but find none of their Constitutions suitable to our circumstances.

In this situation of this Assembly, groping as it were in the dark to find political truth, and scarce able to distinguish it when presented to us, how has it happened, Sir, that we have not hitherto once thought of humbly applying to the Father of lights to illuminate our understandings? In the beginning of the contest with Great Britain, when we were sensible of danger, we had daily prayer in this room for the divine protection. Our prayers, Sir, were heard, and they were graciously answered. All of us who were engaged in the struggle must have observed frequent instances of a Superintending providence in our favor. To that kind providence we owe this happy opportunity of consulting in peace on the means of establishing our future national felicity. And have we now forgotten that powerful friend?

I have lived, Sir, a long time, and the longer I live, the more convincing proofs I see of this truth—that God governs in the affairs of men. And if a sparrow cannot fall to the ground without his notice, is it probable that an empire can rise without his aid? We have been assured, Sir, in the sacred writings, that "except the Lord build the House they labour in vain that build it." I firmly believe this; and I also believe that without his concurring aid we shall succeed in this political building no better than the Builders of Babel: We shall be divided by our little partial local interests; our projects will be confounded, and we ourselves shall become a reproach and by-word down to future ages. And what is worse, mankind may hereafter from this unfortunate instance, despair of establishing

Governments by Human Wisdom and leave it to chance,
war and conquest.

I therefore beg leave to move, that henceforth prayers
imploring the assistance of Heaven, and its blessings on
our deliberations, be held in this Assembly every morning
before we proceed to business, and that one or more of the
Clergy of the City be requested to officiate in that service.

As we know, in the end all impasses were broken, compromises on all issues struck, and solutions found. There was what all felt to be a truly remarkable—almost odd—willingness for each side to set aside its concerns for the good of the whole. The spirit of selflessness and compromise that came over this body of opinionated, brilliant, and principled men was in the end sufficient for them to ratify the great document called the Constitution.

But we should understand that those who were participants in these proceedings marveled at what had happened. George Washington wrote about it in a letter to his friend, the Marquis de Lafayette:

It appears to me, then, little short of a miracle, that the
Delegates from so many different States (which States you
know are also different from each other in their manners,
circumstances, and prejudices) would unite in forming a
system of national Government, so little liable to well
founded objections.

James Madison was even more amazed:

The real wonder is that so many difficulties should have been surmounted, and surmounted with a unanimity almost as unprecedented as it must have been unexpected. It is impossible for any man of candor to reflect on this circumstance without partaking of the astonishment. It is impossible for the man of pious reflection not to perceive in it a finger of that Almighty hand which has been so frequently and signally extended to our relief in the critical stages of the revolution.

It is also extraordinary to think that if the fifty-five men gathered in the summer of 1787 had failed, or had waited to gather a few years later, the difficulties would have been that much more insurmountable. For one thing, the French Revolution, which was just about to begin, would bitterly divide many of the founders, most notably John Adams and Thomas Jefferson. That summer represented a swiftly closing window of opportunity into an unprecedented world, a world of ordered liberty that could last and would last, and somehow the founders got through it just in time. Somehow. Why is it too much for us to suppose—as Franklin, Washington, Adams, and so many others did—that the finger of the Almighty might indeed have been involved? This was an idea that did not die with the founders but lived and was kindled afresh by Abraham Lincoln, who faced obstacles every bit as difficult as what the founders faced, and who came to the same conclusions about how they must be surmounted.

"THE ALMOST CHOSEN PEOPLE"

On the morning of February 20, 1861, in New York City, the soon-to-be inaugurated Abraham Lincoln met with a ninety-four-year-old man named Joshua Dewey. Dewey was born in 1767 and had been a drummer boy in the revolution. He had voted in every presidential election since the first, when George Washington was elected in 1789. None of this was lost on Lincoln, whose sense of history and of America's place in history was formidable. In fact, no other president can be said to have had anything to equal it. So for Lincoln, on the way to his own inaugural, to meet this man would have meant a great deal, and that the meeting took place at Lincoln's hotel, the Astor House, just a few blocks north of the very spot where the old Federal Hall had stood—and where Washington had been inaugurated— would have powerfully underscored the significance of it. Lincoln understood that these links with the past were more than affectations or conceits. There was something to them. He clearly believed in destiny—national and personal—and he took it seriously, especially as he was facing the unspeakably grim prospect of a national civil war. With each day that now passed bringing him closer to Washington, DC, and to the day he would take office, the burden of what he was facing grew.

And as if to endow him with the appearance of gravitas necessary for the office ahead, a beard grew too. The idea for it had been suggested to him a few months earlier in a letter written by an eleven-year-old girl named Grace Bedell. Lincoln met Grace Bedell the day before he met Joshua Dewey. Bedell later recalled that the great man sat down next to her on the train station platform and said, "Gracie, look at my whiskers. I have been growing them for you." "Then he kissed me," she said. "I never saw him again." Grace lived until 1936.

The day after his meeting with Joshua Dewey, Lincoln's train took him further along the journey to Washington, DC, stopping in Trenton, New Jersey, where he addressed the New Jersey State Senate. What he said in that speech bears quoting at length, because in these words Lincoln clearly expresses his sense of history and of his place in it.

> *Mr. President and Gentlemen of the Senate of the State of New-Jersey:*
>
> *I am very grateful to you for the honorable reception of which I have been the object. I cannot but remember the place that New-Jersey holds in our early history. In the early Revolutionary struggle, few of the States among the old Thirteen had more of the battle-fields of the country within their limits than old New-Jersey. May I be pardoned if,*

upon this occasion, I mention that away back in my child-
hood, the earliest days of my being able to read, I got hold
of a small book, such a one as few of the younger members
have ever seen, "Weem's Life of Washington." I remember
all the accounts there given of the battle fields and struggles
for the liberties of the country, and none fixed themselves
upon my imagination so deeply as the struggle here at
Trenton, New-Jersey. The crossing of the river; the contest
with the Hessians; the great hardships endured at that
time, all fixed themselves on my memory more than any
single revolutionary event; and you all know, for you have
all been boys, how these early impressions last longer than
any others. I recollect thinking then, boy even though I
was, that there must have been something more than
common that those men struggled for; that something
even more than National Independence; that something
that held out a great promise to all the people of the world
for all time to come. . . .

These are extraordinary words, hardly what one expects to
hear from a bureaucrat or legislator or lawyer or politician. Lincoln hallows the memory of those who have gone before him in
fighting for "something more than common," and he rightly
says that their struggle was not merely about achieving national
independence. Others could do that and would do that, but this
was far more than that. This, he said, "held out a great promise

to all the people of the world [for] all time to come." What a statement! And then he ends with what has rightly become a famous passage:

> *I am exceedingly anxious that this Union, the Constitution, and the liberties of the people shall be perpetuated in accordance with the original idea for which that struggle was made, and I shall be most happy indeed if I shall be an humble instrument in the hands of the Almighty, and of this, his almost chosen people, for perpetuating the object of that great struggle.*

Arguably our greatest president drew upon his childhood memories of heroic tales of America's past in facing probably the grimmest prospect any U.S. president ever has faced. Those old stories meant much to him and informed his own sense of the country and her destiny. As I have said, reading and knowing those heroic stories is an important part of what it means to be an American. But in the final sentence Lincoln sums up what he thinks of America and the American people. It is there that he calls us God's "almost chosen people," a phrase that is a sparkling distillation of the ideas behind what we have called American exceptionalism. This is because it makes clear that Lincoln did not think America's exceptionalism a mere accident of history. Indeed, a few lines earlier he makes it clear that he sees our special role in history much as John Winthrop saw it and as many men in the two centuries connecting them saw it: as nothing less than a holy calling. But this is the point. We were called by God not for ourselves but for the whole world. What we did on our shores would be and was witnessed by the whole world, and it was for them that we did what we did. In what we were doing and in who we would become, we would be a promise to the whole world of a new way of living, something they could reach for as well, something we must help them to do, as we are able. In this way of seeing ourselves, we were to be a sign to the whole world beyond ourselves.

But also at the center of this idea of being called by God is a humility and even a sadness—both of which can be said to characterize Lincoln's attitude toward his office and his role in history. But as he said in his speech, it was all for something "that held out a great promise to all the people of the world [for] all time to come." He understood that America was indeed great, but precisely because she did not merely exist for herself. She was exceptional because she pointed outward, beyond herself. Her place in history was always to reach beyond herself— and once she forgot this, she would cease to be America. In reminding the men of the New Jersey legislature of their common history, this is the point Lincoln was making.

We are not here talking about the contested and controversial idea of "Manifest Destiny," nor merely of noblesse oblige, but of something far more serious, of something that is even sacred. Lincoln felt that America had been called by God to fulfill a role and to perform a duty for the rest of the world. It was not something to be giddy about. Far from it. He understood that to be chosen by God—as the Jews had been chosen by God, and as the prophets had been chosen by God, and as the Messiah had been chosen by God—was something that was a profound and sacred and even terrifying obligation. One would not wish to be chosen, but one might nobly be willing to be chosen, despite the suffering that it would surely entail. So Lincoln more than any president had a sense of this and of the great history that preceded him in all that he was doing. He seemed almost to know that the country he would soon lead was being called onto the bloody battlefields of a civil war, so he was sober and sad, and yet not discouraged. Rather it seems that what he knew of history and of America's destiny was a deep encouragement to him in facing this great trial.

Of course, the idea that God had chosen this nation for great things does not sit comfortably with modern sensibilities. Nonetheless we must see that for Lincoln and for so many others it was inescapable.

Just as many believe the Jews had been chosen by God to bring his Messiah into the world, and through that Messiah to lead the whole world to the God they worshipped, so for Lincoln America had been chosen by God to bring a new kind of nation into the world, and through that nation to lead the whole world to take part in that experiment in liberty for all. This was not an idea that was much questioned, though it has certainly been misunderstood and misapplied. But for those, like Lincoln, who perceived it rightly, the only thing to question was whether we could acquit ourselves as God wished us to do in this mission to the rest of the world, whether we would be worthy of our role as a "shining city on a hill" and would use our position to lead others to the liberty and blessings that we already enjoyed.

We may also remind ourselves that for Lincoln and the others who understood this the great responsibility was not merely toward others but toward God. For them it was God who had the idea in the first place and who had called America as a people to accomplish this task. It was for his purposes in history, to bless the whole world with the freedoms we had enjoyed. So the idea that America was to be a blessing to the rest of the world and to the future was inextricably intertwined with the God of the Bible, whom these people believed had led them to do what they were doing.

We may need to remind ourselves that Governor John Winthrop of the Massachusetts Bay Colony was not a mere political figure. He was first and foremost the leader of a distinctly Christian group. Its members were not only escaping religious persecution in Europe but were trying to set up a new model of community, one in which mutual charity would be at the core. They would care for one another. The rich would lift up the poor. This is something that resonates with us today in large part because Winthrop and his fellow shipmates were successful. What they did shone so brightly that their distinctly biblical model carried on beyond the Massachusetts Bay Colony and into the United States of America, however imperfectly. In fact, it was so very successful that we no longer see it for what it is: a distinctly Christian idea, one that was utterly alien to all other societies of that day. It was certainly not the norm or the standard in the ostensibly Christian nation of Britain, which they were fleeing. Indeed, it was not the norm or the standard anywhere else on the globe. It was something utterly new and untried.

But this is inescapably at the heart of America. We cannot deny this any more than we can deny the sins of America. This unavoidable aspect of who we are has been acknowledged and reasserted time and again, from Winthrop through the founders through Lincoln and all the way into the present.

But we might well ask ourselves, if arguably our greatest president was brimming with this sense of America's calling, and if this idea has carried forward to some extent in the speeches of presidents as recent as Kennedy and Reagan, how is it that it is today, in the second decade of the twenty-first century, largely forgotten? How did we as a nation go from being serious about this idea—and at times even overzealous in it—to having largely dismissed it, along with slavery, as an embarrassing relic of our past?

The answer may be found in a speech that Lincoln gave in 1837 at the Young Men's Lyceum of Springfield when he was just twenty-eight years old. He makes a sober assessment of our stature in the world at that time and, after doing that, asks from where our undoing might come.

We find ourselves in the peaceful possession, of the fairest portion of the earth, as regards extent of territory, fertility of soil, and salubrity of climate. We find ourselves under the government of a system of political institutions, conducing more essentially to the ends of civil and religious liberty, than any of which the history of former times tells us. We, when mounting the stage of existence, found ourselves the legal inheritors of these fundamental blessings.

Shall we expect some transatlantic military giant to step the ocean and crush us at a blow? Never! All the armies of Europe, Asia, and Africa combined, with all the treasure of the earth (our own excepted) in their military chest, with a Bonaparte for a commander, could not by force take a drink from the Ohio or make a track on the Blue Ridge in a trial of a thousand years. At what point then is the approach of danger to be expected? I answer. If it ever reach us it must spring up amongst us; it cannot come from abroad. If destruction be our lot we must ourselves be its author and finisher. As a nation of freemen we must live through all time or die by suicide.

So if we turn away from our calling—whether intentionally or merely by forgetting what that calling is—we commit suicide. And if we turn away from the moral law, we forfeit the blessings of God.

Lincoln knew when he faced the crisis of the Civil War that what America was doing had everything to do with that moral law. Could we keep it and continue to be favored by God? That was the question he was trying to help Americans understand and answer. The republic depended on it. Either we would turn from the great sin of slavery forever, or we would perish. We were a country on a mission to the whole world, but first we must get our own house in order. If we could not survive the agony of so doing, we would surely fail in our God-given mission to the world beyond our shores. But how were we to do that then—and how can we do it now? What have we forgotten that we must remember again?

SEVEN

Loving America

If you don't boast about your home, it will
fall down and crush you.

— Greek proverb

Twelve days after meeting with the nonagenarian Revolutionary War veteran Joshua Dewey, Lincoln was in Washington, DC, to be inaugurated on the steps of the United States Capitol. Since his election in November, seven states had seceded from the Union. As far as they were concerned, they were no longer part of the United States. If the United States under Lincoln's leadership would take any steps to bring them back into the Union, the South would go to war. What Lincoln was proposing to say would need to bear the weight of history.

We know that the speech he had with him was composed back in Springfield, in the back of his brother-in-law's store. What did it say? The few who had read it were sworn to secrecy. On March 4, 1861, the day of Lincoln's inauguration had come.

"MYSTIC CHORDS OF MEMORY"

Abraham Lincoln had been elected the sixteenth president on November 10, 1860. Five weeks from that inauguration, in March, would mark the outbreak of the Civil War. It's clear from what Lincoln says in his speech that things in the country were at a breaking point. He understands that he is facing the terrible prospect of an unspeakably bloody war, the unprecedented horror of Americans killing Americans en masse. But on that day no one's life was in more danger than Lincoln's. Horace Greeley, the editor of the *New York Tribune*, was seated right behind the new president and wrote that throughout Lincoln's speech he was "expecting to hear its delivery arrested by the crack of a rifle aimed at his heart."

The tension in the country and especially there in the nation's capital was at a high pitch. Because all of this happened so long ago, we can hardly imagine what it must have seemed like to those present. We have heard over and over and over about brother being pitted against brother, to the point that it ceases to mean anything. Time has rendered these things into clichés and bromides. But that day it was all palpable. Sharpshooters were on roofs in the vicinity and rumors of plots to assassinate or kidnap the president circulated widely.

Lincoln's speech was calculated to face the situation head-on, and to assure the other side that he would not use the powers of the federal government to attack them. But in the final words of the speech he takes everything a step further. In the speech Lincoln tries to assure those on the other side of things that they are not enemies but friends. In the final words of the speech, in its most famous passage, he is looking almost prophetically at the landscape far beyond the smoke and carnage of the four-year war ahead, toward a time and a place that would exist only after he is himself murdered by an assassin.

"I am lo[a]th to close," he writes. "We are not enemies, but friends. We must not be enemies. Though passion may have strained, it must not break our bonds of affection." He then delivers the speech's final words, a passage that has rightly become famous. "The mystic chords of memory," he says, "stretching from every battle-field, and patriot grave, to every living heart and hearthstone, all over this broad land, will yet swell the chorus of the Union, when again touched, as surely they will be, by the better angels of our nature."

It is undeniably beautiful and moving. But what are those "mystic chords of memory"? Lincoln is speaking of something ineffable, something beyond mere logic or law. After all, what can something as poetic as "mystic chords of memory" have to do with the Constitution? Lincoln is speaking of the thing that makes a people a people, that causes them to be something more than individuals living on the same piece of land or individuals under the same governmental authority and beholden to the same laws. What he speaks of has to do with a deep feeling that is yet itself much more than a mere feeling. It is a uniquely human thing that cannot be put into a document or written into laws. In fact, it is something upon which all the sacred documents and laws themselves depend, without which they are absurd.

So what exactly are these "mystic chords of memory" that stretch "from every battle-field, and patriot grave"? Lincoln believed that it was this that made us a people, more than our form of government and our laws, and he believed that it was this that would save us in the end, would make us a people again, on the other side of the hatred and death. Guns and cannons could save America only for a short period, and it would take those "mystic chords" to heal its wounds after the battles and bloodshed. Without them there could be no union, save in name only.

The people of the South would eventually concede defeat and would have to abide by the laws of the government from which they had tried to secede. But they must do this voluntarily, at least at some point. The Union could not hold together long if not for that desire to abide by something, which could never really be forced. The Union was no dictatorship, and the

United States was not some empire with a tyrant at its helm, despite what some—including John Wilkes Booth—thought at the time.

In his first inaugural address, the onetime country lawyer Abraham Lincoln moved beyond the law. What he says in that passage is not merely legal. It is, indeed, poetic. In a day when politicians have speeches crafted for them by teams of Beltway speechwriters, it is difficult to fathom that we once elected a self-taught leader who grew up reading Parson Weems and the King James Bible by firelight in a rural cabin with a dirt floor and who was capable of writing lines as eternal as those written by the greatest of poets.

Lincoln was more than a legislator and politician; he was a poet and a prophet. His words were lapidary when they came from his pen and when he spoke them, and they became so literally when years later they were inscribed on stones for millions of Americans to read. Lincoln shows us in these and other words that "we the people" are more than a voting bloc. There is something far deeper at work, something revealed by these "mystic chords of memory."

We cannot avoid it: Lincoln is talking about love of country. That's what the appeal in his inaugural speech is about. It is about seeing beyond policy proposals and other details. It is about coming together as a people over those things that truly bind us together. Lincoln is saying that love of country is necessary, that America cannot and will not survive without it. But who can deny that this idea has all these years later fallen on hard times? Who among us can anymore even say what love of country is?

LOVING AMERICA

When facing the death of the nation he clearly loved, our greatest president declared that it was those "mystic chords of memory" that would hold us together, beyond the vast battlefields of horrors that lay ahead. The greatest test of our republic would rely not merely on our political institutions and on the great leader who was speaking those words but on something else. It would depend on our love for America. The ineffable idea of love for America would be the thing to heal us up beyond our difficulties and carry us together, North and South, ex-slave and free, into the future. What are we to make of this: that love of country was, in the estimation of Lincoln, crucial to the survival of America? Did Lincoln not himself earnestly believe that? Was he merely calculating that this sentiment would operate on the hearts of that generation, a generation susceptible to such ideas? Or perhaps he did sincerely believe it, but we do not, in our more sophisticated age? Or is this idea of loving one's country rather an eternal verity that must be remembered and relearned, lest we fail to survive our current trials, which are great? Is it possible that unless we remember and relearn how to love our country that it will die by suicide, as Lincoln warned—or prophesied—in his 1837 speech at the Springfield Young Men's Lyceum?

Lincoln's other statements would lead us to conclude that he dearly and deeply believed what he was saying about love of country, and simple logic obliges us to face the idea that nothing has changed to make this idea—this requirement—any less important to the survival of our country today. But perhaps in order for us to remember how to love our country and to relearn how to do so, we need to ask ourselves exactly what it means to love one's country. Perhaps it is our understanding of this idea itself that has changed.

The first question to ask is how can we plausibly be expected to "love" a country we now know to be guilty of so many things? Ronald Reagan once said, "If we forget what we did, we won't know who we are." This is true. I've said from this book's beginning that seeing ourselves as we are is vital if we are to "keep the republic" as Franklin enjoined us to do that day in Philadelphia. But knowing who we are means we must know both the positive things and the negative.

Since roughly the 1960s the negative things have come to the fore in unprecedented ways. As the war in Vietnam escalated, we increasingly began to see ourselves in a negative light: as a people who had oppressed our native peoples, and who had tolerated the great moral evil of slavery, and who had allowed horrible racial injustices to continue long after that institution had been abolished. We had denied women the vote for well over a century and had gotten involved in a war that for the first time forced many of us to question whether we could be seen as the "good guy" on the world stage. In many ways, seeing these bad things about ourselves was an extraordinarily positive development, in that we ought to own up to and deal with the worst of what we've done and who we have been.

But the real problems arose when we somehow split into two camps over this and fell into a perpetual ideological battle. One side seemed only to be able to see the bad things America had done, and seemed to have become enamored of the negative narrative that cast us as the great villain on the world stage; and the other side seemed only to be able to see the faults with that narrative, and seemed to have become enamored of the positive narrative that cast us as the great savior of the world. This perpetual ideological battle has become a dangerous thing for America and for the world both. To truly love America, one must somehow see both sides simultaneously.

The two warring sides came into being during the time of the Vietnam War, when the negative, critical voices reached a fever pitch. Those who were upset about the criticisms and saw them as nakedly unpatriotic raised their hackles and defiantly coined the slogan "America, Love It or Leave It." This expresses one side of the deep misunderstanding about what it means to love one's country. Those on the other side of the divide—those who were criticizing our country in a way that often veered into hating her—were expressing the other. And there we have been, generally speaking, ever since. It is one of history's greatest tragedies, not least because it has serious international ramifications. This inability to see both sides simultaneously, to love the one and hate the other, has been dramatic.

We see 1920s photographs of lynchings, with smiling people, young and old, standing around the tortured body of an African American, and we must acknowledge this as part of our history. But we must also acknowledge our most heroic moments without waving them off as rare anomalies or as mere hypocrisy. When we see the shameful way Andrew Jackson treated Native Americans, we must accept this as part of our history, but we must also see the courage and faith of those priests and missionaries who were tortured and killed for trying to bring their faith to some of those Native Americans. We must remember the My Lai massacre, but we must also remember when firefighters wearing heavy gear marched into the flaming towers of the World Trade Center to their deaths. Heroism and ignominy both are part of our history. The only question is whether, having seen both, we can repent of the one and rejoice and be inspired by the other. Or whether we will let one of them tempt us so far away from the other that we have a deeply distorted view.

What is the true view of America and how can we see it? We must also ask—if we believe God exists or might exist—what his view of America would be. And what does God think about patriotism and love of country?

Before we answer those questions, let's agree that we may

legitimately wonder how one can "love" a country that once en-slaved millions and profited from that inhuman and degrading practice? But we should immediately remember that Lincoln was more aware than we are of the moral horror of slavery, and he seems to have gotten past that difficulty to love America and see the need for other Americans to love her. But perhaps our love of America is prevented by other things? Perhaps it's much more recent racial sins that rankle us. Or perhaps our global sins seem more of a barrier to loving our country, which is today so much larger and richer and more powerful than it ever was in the mid-dle of the nineteenth century. For some it might be our more recent legalization of abortion. There are unfortunately many reasons we might cite against loving our country.

Or perhaps, as I have said before, the very idea of loving one's country is outdated. Perhaps we think that it's possible to move past such parochial notions? Aren't we called to love everyone and to love other countries as much as our own? Isn't loving what is one's own simply a form of selfishness and tribalism? Shouldn't we rather think of ourselves as "one world" under God rather than as "one nation" under God?

The shortest answer to these questions is yes and no. That's because when Jesus said we are to love our neighbors as our-selves, he was assuming that we already loved ourselves. He as-sumed that loving ourselves—and our family and tribe and those things that are near and familiar to us—was natural and not to be scorned. The Greek proverb "If you don't boast about your home, it will fall down and crush you" makes this implicit assumption an explicit warning. It envisions the error of failing to take sufficient pride in what is ours, and it also warns that to do this is to commit something like suicide. We may again remember Lincoln's prescient Lyceum speech of 1837. Somehow it seems that we are called to take pride in what is ours, and to love it—up to a point.

So yes, our pride has limits. Our national pride should not veer into jingoism or nationalism. That can lead us badly astray too. Yet Jesus's command and this Greek proverb both imply that a healthy pride is necessary and that we cannot suffer only from too much pride but also from too little. Both seem to suggest that if we don't love ourselves and what is ours, and take pride in ourselves and what is ours, we will be in no position to love others or other things. If we do not first take appropriate pride in ourselves, we cannot extend our pride to others. If I hate myself, how can I ever take real pride in the accomplishments of someone else? And if I hate my country—or at least fail to love it—how can I extend anything worthy to someone in another country? If I want to give money to others, don't I first have to possess it myself? Isn't hating oneself or hating one's country in fact a kind of reverse pride, one that puts too much focus on ourselves at the expense of a more balanced and gracious view, the kind of view we are called to have toward others? If God calls us to love our enemies, can't we apply that to ourselves as well, to treat ourselves with love, despite knowing the worst of our own sins?

But we are getting ahead of ourselves. To be proud of one's home, one's family, one's village, one's city, and one's country is something that from the beginning of history has been somehow understood as vital. It is one of the universal hallmarks of human behavior. In another exhortation Jesus called his followers to "do unto others as you would have others do unto you," which, of course, presupposes a healthy kind of self-interest. But in the last decades in the United States of America and in other parts of the West, this fundamental idea has been forgotten. We have bought into the false choice of either loving our country or loving others, when it seems that we cannot properly love others and help others unless we love ourselves and help ourselves first. If we truly love others and want to help others, we must see that the two are inextricably intertwined.

So can we take a healthy pride in ourselves again, if we understand what that really means? Can Americans see our way back to loving ourselves in a way that at its core desires to extend that love to others? Perhaps we first have to understand a bit more about what love is—and is not.

WHAT IS LOVE?

One way of understanding what love is and what it means to love is to say that to love something is to see it as we think God would see it—rather than as we, fallen human beings, are inclined to see it. To love something is to see in it the hope and the promise that are in it, which our cynical, tired selves cannot see but which by God's grace we can see. We do not fail to see the sins and failings, but we also see past them to the hope and the promise. Seeing the sins and failings is therefore not final and fatalistic. We see them but we see beyond them to the possibilities of goodness and forgiveness and redemption. We recognize that "the story's not over." We see the hope on the other side of where we are.

So when God in the Bible tells us that we are to love our enemies, he is not telling us to love what is evil, or to love the evil in our enemies. He is telling us to love what is beyond that, to love the goodness in them that he sees and that he put there. He is telling us that if we love that good thing, it will grow. If we look at that—via the "better angels of our nature"—we will feed it and thereby also starve what is evil. In other words, what we love we change toward the good—by loving it. That is the only path forward, if we care about what is good. We must choose what we look at; and we must choose what we look beyond. But if our focus is on what is ugly and evil and dark, we will strangely strengthen the ugly and evil and dark.

To see what this really means, we must only think about love in personal terms. If I have a son or a daughter or a spouse or a parent or another relative or a friend, I will eventually see things in their behavior that I perhaps perceive as troubling, even as out-and-out wrong. How do I deal with that? There are a few typical ways. One of them is to home in on those problems by constantly pointing them out and criticizing that person so that the person feels unloved. Another is to be unable to divorce the person from their behavior—to say, in effect, *Whatever that person does is correct. If I love them I must accept them 'as they are.'* We can hate the sin and hate the sinner or we can love the sin and love the sinner. Both are wrong. There is a third way. What if we love the sinner but hate the sin? Isn't that what we're supposed to do?

What if we treat someone as though he were the way we wished him to be? What if I treat a child as though he were trustworthy and dependable? On some level I am speaking those qualities into that child. This is not merely wishful thinking—although it can devolve into that—but practically speaking we must concede that if we treat someone as though they are good and dependable and honest, we are to some extent helping that person to step into those qualities.

Conversely, if we treat someone with constant suspicion and criticism, we are helping them in the other direction, to see themselves as "untrustworthy" or as generally bad. We all know that if a parent says to a child, "You'll never amount to anything," that parent plays a part in making sure that that child will never amount to anything. Conversely, if one says to a child, "You are wonderful and will grow to do great things," one is helping that child to step in that other direction. Neither statement guarantees the outcome, but what we say to someone and how we treat them inevitably has an effect in one direction or another.

When we behave this way, when we refuse to love someone, and deliberately withhold our love from them, we want them to feel it. Some would say that in this we are "judging" them. But in a way we are also cursing them. Instead of calling them higher, we are condemning them to stay where they are, in their faults and sins and shortcomings. We won't acknowledge the best in them, because we want to make them pay for their bad behavior first. We are seeking to punish them, but in doing this we are feeding the very thing we wish to starve and condemning them to be their worst forever.

To love someone is to see the best in them and to act toward them as though they were that best. To call them higher. To treat them with respect and love is to call them to be worthy of that respect and that love. And we can say that to love someone is not to avoid seeing their flaws, but to avoid so focusing on them that the person gets a feeling of hopelessness about changing them.

Those who have adopted an "America is the problem" attitude, who have characterized America as an imperialistic "world bully," are simply wrong. They are no different from those who would say America has no flaws and can do no wrong. Both are fundamental misunderstandings of what it means to love one's country and to be a good citizen who is helping lead one's nation in the right direction.

In John Winthrop's sermon aboard the *Arbella* in 1630, he was saying that we have a burden to carry, a responsibility to the world. If we get it wrong, God will judge us for that. But he was setting forth a model of how we can and should get it right. By saying that we were a shining "city on a hill" and telling us that we must work toward that ideal, he was speaking to the "better angels of our nature" and therefore speaking in a way that called us in that direction.

So those of us who have adopted a cynical view of this nation and who have a dour, negative view of it are doing our part in making sure that our negative view of America is what America becomes. Somehow, with our views and words and actions, we are guaranteeing that America does not become what she should. You might even say that when we do this we are cursing America, in our own way making sure she fails. Of course, this is the opposite of love and it is wrong. It not only harms America but harms the world beyond America, which, as we have said, America exists to bless.

On the other hand, those who in response to this negative attitude toward America swerve across the road into the ditch on the other side are equally wrong. To pretend that America can do no wrong is just like the parent who refuses to deal with the issues that are clearly problems in their child's life. To so ignore them that one helps them to continue is also cursing that child, that country. Both sides are not saying "God bless America" but are really calling on God to curse America, a country that Lincoln called "the best great hope of Earth." To love America is something else altogether—and if we are to keep the promise of America, it is necessary.

But we must also remember that to love someone or something is to call that someone or something to love. The very idea of love is a self-sacrificial action that calls the object of our love toward self-sacrifice. So that in loving America we are embodying her original intentions—we are indeed being America at her best—and in doing so we are calling her to be her best, to be focused on doing all she can to fulfill the great promise to which God himself has called her in bringing her into existence and shepherding her through trials and tribulations all these decades and centuries—and now.

So we know that we must love our country. But how?

There are numerous ways. Of course, one of those ways has to do with telling the darker truths about her, as I've said, but only if we do so in a way that is not ultimately hopeless and cynical but that moves toward hope, toward fixing the problem, whatever that problem might be. And one way we can do that is through the arts. Since the sixties most artistic expressions concerning America have fallen into the hopeless and cynical rut I've mentioned, so it's usually easiest to find art from before that time—poems like "Paul Revere's Ride" and paintings like *Washington Crossing the Delaware* and sculptures like the magnificent Iwo Jima statue in our nation's capital. Generally we've erred so far in the direction of telling the dark truths about America that as a corrective we might do well to focus on her positive attributes. But this isn't to say there isn't room for criticism. On the contrary. One film that is critical of America, but that does so in a way that is inspiring and hopeful, pointing her back to her true self rather than bludgeoning her with the sins of her past, is Frank Capra's *Mr. Smith Goes to Washington*.

MR. SMITH GOES TO WASHINGTON

In this 1939 film an everyman, played by Jimmy Stewart, is by some fluke elected to the Senate, where he confronts the entrenched and corrupt politics that are there. He is clearly intended to represent all Americans, and Capra gives him the name "Mr. Smith," just in case we are not clear on that point. In fact, to underscore what we are to think of him, his name in the movie is "Jefferson Smith." The movie was nominated for eleven Academy Awards and is now regarded as a classic American film, as it should be. It is a glorious paean to our country at its best, and it's a movie every American should see.

But just to show how far America has veered in seventy-five years, we may recall that at the time of its release, the film was seen as too critical of America. The head of the Hays Office at that time, Joseph Breen, worried about "the generally unflattering portrayal of our system of Government, which might well lead to such a picture being considered, both here, and more particularly abroad, as a covert attack on the Democratic form of government." He actually demanded the movie make clear that "the Senate is made up of a group of fine, upstanding citizens, who labor long and tirelessly for the best interests of the nation."

JFK's father, Joseph P. Kennedy—then the U.S. ambassador to Great Britain—argued it would give comfort to our enemies abroad in its criticism of our government. After the film was released, he recommended the film not be released in Europe because it might damage "American prestige" there. But contrary to such fears, the film was actually banned in Germany, Russia, Spain, and Italy. That's because totalitarians, communists, and fascists like Hitler, Stalin, Franco, and Mussolini rightly saw it—with its healthy self-criticism of the American government—as a boon to America and as dangerously threatening to their own repressive views.

Today, of course, the film is in some places thought too pro-American, too idealistic, and too heroic and hopeful, even corny. Those who see America as the problem in the world don't point to *Mr. Smith Goes to Washington* as the antidote. They have moved far beyond that level of open-eyed hopefulness, feeling that America as she was conceived is somehow irredeemable and so flawed that we should be pointed not back to our roots but away from them. For them such corruption in our system is a given, power politics are part of the dirty game that must be played, and one must cynically accept them and play to win.

REMEMBRANCE AND RITUAL

Another way we can love America is through remembrance and ritual. In fact, rituals often exist specifically to help us remember. In the Old Testament, God repeatedly instructs the Israelites to do things on certain dates and to create monuments, precisely so that they will never forget what they have experienced. He knows that if they remember these things it will be that much harder for them to stray, and so every year, among other things, Jews celebrate Passover, with many specific rituals about how and what to eat and what prayers to recite. Every culture must have rituals and in America we have a few, but even in celebrating them we often forget why we are celebrating them. Some people think the Fourth of July is when we celebrate firecrackers and have barbecues, forgetting the reason we explode firecrackers and have barbecues in the first place. Making every Fourth of July, or every Thanksgiving, or every Memorial Day, a day on which we specifically remember something historical about that day would be a way to begin. Perhaps every April 18 we might ask children to recite portions of "Paul Revere's Ride" and talk about it. On the Fourth of July we might have children recite portions of the Declaration of Independence. On February 12 we might do something to remember Abraham Lincoln and on February 22 we might do something to remember George Washington. We should do these things in our communities, in front of our town halls, and in front of our libraries, and in our churches and synagogues and mosques, and of course we must do them in our schools. Doing such things in our schools is perhaps the principal way we can help teach the next generation what it means to love our country. In fact, I still remember something that I did on June 14, 1973.

I was just shy of my tenth birthday and our fifth-grade teacher, Mrs. Saul, told us that we were all going outside to celebrate Flag Day. I'd never heard of Flag Day before. Later I learned that the Revolutionary Congress adopted the Stars and Stripes as the official flag of the new country on June 14, 1777, and the date has been designated Flag Day ever since. So we marched out of the classroom to the flagpole in front of the school. We were a small class of fifteen and we stood around the flagpole in a circle as Mr. Piccarello, who was my trumpet teacher, joined us. I was surprised to see that he did not have a brass trumpet, as I did, but a beautiful silver cornet. He put it to his lips, and as we stood around the flagpole he played "My Country, 'Tis of Thee," and we sang:

> *My Country, 'tis of thee,*
> *Sweet land of liberty,*
> *Of thee I sing!*
> *Land where our fathers died,*
> *Land of the Pilgrims' pride*
> *From every mountainside,*
> *Let freedom ring!*

After that he played taps, which is often played at flag cere-
monies, and we listened. It was sonorous and solemn and beautiful. Those moments around the flagpole on that June day over
forty years ago so pricked my heart that I still think of them
with the deepest reverence. It seems to me like a holy memory,
like something from another time, from an innocent time beyond this world, from the golden world that is childhood. But
what were we doing there that day? I realize now that we were
participating in a ritual and I realize that, like all rituals, it was
designed to evoke something in us. But what? I think now I
know. We were being taught to love our country.

There was something about what we were doing that told us
all that somehow this was important. It was telling us that that
flag there is more than a flag. It is more than a red-white-and-
blue banner that droops or waves. It is a sacred symbol that points
toward something beyond itself, that points to the real thing that
it represents, to America, the country that we've been learning
about in this school year, the country that was "born in liberty"
and for which all of those heroes fought and died and which you
are now entrusted to keep. Nothing of the kind was said in words,
but it didn't need to be said. On levels that are beyond words it
was communicated, and without words we took it in.

There weren't many more moments like this in my education. Already by 1973 these sorts of patriotic rituals were on
their way out, especially in public schools and especially in the
North. But Mrs. Saul had started teaching in the 1930s, so she

had likely been doing this for four decades, and now, in her last year of teaching, we fifteen students got to experience the very tail end of what one might call a Norman Rockwell, Frank Capra view of America, of a nation made up mainly of small towns, where people were proud to gather around flagpoles and to celebrate our common history and heritage.

Those rituals were making us part of something, linking us to all those around the country that Flag Day and other Flag Days and other patriotic days throughout the nation's history. When we were older we would think of this day and it would mean something to us. It was one of those "mystic chords of memory" of which Lincoln spoke, that bound us to others in a way that was beautiful and true. The magic of it is that you cannot boil it down to something. You cannot reduce it. It was not indoctrination. It was beautiful, pointing to something beyond itself, pointing to something noble and true and eternal. We were being taught to love America.

Our affections were being shaped and directed. We were being pointed to something noble and ennobling: our sense of ourselves as a great nation worth celebrating, a nation whose ideas are worth spreading around the globe. Which brings me back to another idea, that our love for what is good in ourselves personally and what is good in our country actually causes us to love what is good in others and in other countries. That is the paradox of true love. To love the goodness in any one thing is to love goodness itself. To love one thing to the exclusion of the goodness in other things is not to love that one thing at all but to make a false idol of it and to hate real goodness.

MEMORIZING POETRY

Almost four years after that June day around the flagpole I found myself celebrating another national ritual, although this time it had to do with my Greek background. Each March 25, Greeks around the world celebrate their independence and freedom from the Ottoman Empire, which for nearly four centuries subjugated them and made passing on their Greek Orthodox Christian faith terribly difficult. So for Greeks that date is like our July Fourth, and in most Greek Orthodox churches there is a celebration on the Sunday near that date in which the children recite poems they've been tasked with memorizing. I, being thirteen and known to be good in school, was given "*O Gero Demos*" to learn. When I saw the poem, my heart sank. It was very long. Memorizing it would be an agony.

But my father would get me up early in the morning before school every weekday, and we'd sit on the couch in the living room and work on it. My father broke the poem up into sections, so the idea was to simply learn one section at a time. That he would get up early to do this with me says something about him as a father that I'm sure I failed to appreciate at the time. I seem to remember so little of it, all those hours we spent.

What I do remember distinctly is that every now and again my father would be explaining what some lines in the poem meant—or he might be reciting a portion of it for me—and he would get choked up and stop talking and look away with tears in his eyes. I was, of course, embarrassed, as any thirteen-year-old would be, weathering the awkward seconds of silence, not knowing what to do with myself as my father took the time to gather himself. But some of my embarrassment came from feeling inadequate, from feeling that whatever it was that he was experiencing was somehow beyond me, that I wasn't yet able to understand it, although I knew that I should understand it—that it was something powerful and noble and meaningful that I didn't grasp yet, because I hadn't suffered. I felt my callowness in those moments.

My father always choked up when he recited or read the noble words he was reading about people who had given their lives for liberty, who had given their very lives in the service of something greater, for freedom, and whom we were remembering as we sat there on the couch memorizing those lines so that we could celebrate these things as a community in the parish hall of the church on Farview Avenue in Danbury a few weeks hence. And I understood then that this was not some tribalist exercise in which we were merely celebrating Greece and Greek history and Greek accomplishments. On the contrary, what we were celebrating was good and true and beautiful for all people for all time. The freedom of the Greeks from the Ottomans was like our freedom from English tyranny; it was something all people should love and celebrate. It was something universal because in the end it was not about Greece but about the idea of liberty, which is a universal idea, an idea that God has given us as a gift, which it is his will that we have and that we give to others. So really what my father was doing with me in those mornings on the couch was teaching me to love what was beautiful and good and true. And by teaching me to love that through the prism of Greek history, he was helping me to love what was good and true and beautiful in my own country and everywhere.

Years later it occurred to me that I was doing the same thing when I was helping my daughter memorize "Paul Revere's Ride." I was teaching her to love sacrifice and goodness and truth and beauty, and I was teaching her the history of America and therefore teaching her to love America, except this time I was the one on the couch getting choked up. I was the one whose feelings via time and personal suffering had caught up with the stories of selfless suffering and sacrifice toward a greater good for others, for me and my family. I was the one with tears in my eyes, the one pausing to look away to gather myself.

If we are loving what is properly good and true and beautiful, we are ordering our affections against tribalism and jingoism; we are ordering our affections so that they are in line with God's affections, because the selfishness of tribalism and nationalism are the very enemies of what God loves. His love expands ever outward through whatever lens or prism we are using. That is the nature of true love, what the Bible calls *agape,* the self-giving love of God.

In his final Narnia book, *The Last Battle,* C. S. Lewis talks about loving not England but God's England. What is God's idea of England? Because that is what God calls us to love in England. And what is God's idea of America? Because it is that in America and that alone that God calls us—nay, commands us—to love. Because the love of what is good and true and beautiful in anything will become the portal through which we love all that is good and true and beautiful beyond it. If we do not love America and teach our children to love America—as God loves her—we can never love the world beyond our shores and can never teach our children to do the same. And that, precisely, is our promise. That is the promise of America. It is why we came into existence and it is why we have flourished and why we must continue to do so.

This Is America

I'll never forget seeing her. It was sometime during the spring of 2002, just a few months after the 9/11 attacks.

On that terrible day at the dawn of this century darkness in two swift strokes fell over America, casting a palpable pall over our city, one that didn't dissipate for a long, long time. In the first few days after it happened, there was a deeply eerie and unsettling silence over the city, the streets nearly empty as everyone either stayed away from the city or stayed huddled in their apartments, watching the endless news programs that revealed more and more details and horrors and raised more questions and fears. When you passed someone on the strangely empty and quiet streets, as we did, pushing our daughter in her stroller, you wondered if you were together at the end of the world. You exchanged glances that seemed to say: *Yes, we are in this together. We don't know you, but because of this tragedy we feel close to you. We are living through this together, and who knows what lies ahead?*

We learned from the television that the horrible acrid and sweet pink gray smoke that wafted northward four miles into our Thirty-eighth Street apartment windows in the days after the tragedy contained the ashes of nearly three thousand people killed that horrible morning. But even after the smoke dissipated, there remained a tangible tension and a deep sadness, a grief that somehow was always with us. And not far away, at what suddenly everyone was calling Ground Zero, the great wound in the earth gaped and smoked for all to see, whether in person or in the endless television images of it, burning for weeks and even months afterward like some hellish portal to the deepest darkness at the heart of our fallen humanity, a twisted gash in the earth leading down to death. It would be many months before the molten carnage could be cleaned up and taken away, and in the meantime the poisonous smoke and the lingering and festering foulness of it took their toll on everyone. But I didn't realize how it all had affected me personally until some months after.

My wife and our then two-and-a-half-year-old daughter

were traveling to visit my in-laws on the New Jersey Shore, and instead of renting a car, as we usually did, we chose to take the new speed ferry that went from Thirty-fourth Street on the East River to the New Jersey Highlands. After we had settled in our seats with our luggage, I left my wife and daughter and climbed to the upper deck to stand outside and watch the scenery speeding by. The double-hulled ferry took us down the East River and out, out past the tip of Manhattan and the stark double ellipsis in her skyline, until suddenly we were way out in the middle of New York Harbor. That's when I saw her, somehow suddenly.

For some reason I'd almost forgotten that she really existed, the green lady in the harbor, Lady Liberty, bravely holding her golden torch to the world. I was surprised to see her, and I surprised myself too, because I instantly got choked up. But why? It was so visceral and instant that it took me a moment to understand my own reaction. But I realized with tears in my eyes that the reason I had tears in my eyes was that after all that had happened she was still there, still standing there, still graciously welcoming foreigners and outcasts, still holding out her torch to light the way to liberty and hope, just as she had been doing for countless generations. Something about her great dignity and nobility as I saw her on that gorgeous day, after all that had happened, got to me. Her noble dignity and her willingness to stand there and extend that grand and humble and heartfelt invitation to the world, that blazing torch of freedom for all. It broke my heart. And as I stood there at the rail of that ship looking at her, the beauty of that beautiful day itself—the bright blue sky and the golden sunlight—broke my heart.

What is it about the death of innocence? It's sad for someone to die and sadder yet for someone to be killed, but it's always saddest when the one who dies is innocent and beautiful and young. Why does the idea of Snow White seemingly dead in her coffin pierce our hearts, and why did the death of Princess Diana cause such an outpouring of grief across England and the world? When such things happen, it is somehow as if goodness and beauty themselves have been murdered. That the tragedy struck America on such a glorious day, so bright and blue and clear, on that heavenly morning, made it all the more poignant, as if morning and innocence themselves had been attacked—as if the breast of the heartbreakingly beautiful blue sky itself had been pierced with a dagger.

When I think of that morning now, and when I recall the face of the Statue of Liberty, I think of the proud and humble face of Atticus Finch in the movie version of Harper Lee's great American novel *To Kill a Mockingbird*, after he's been confronted and spat upon by the racist Bob Ewell, and I think of how he nobly stands there, willing to take whatever he must for what he knows to be right. And I think of the face of Martin Luther King Jr., dignified and holding out hope in the midst of scorn and darkest hatred. And I think of the brave and youthful face of Nathan Hale on the gallows declaring that he regrets only that he has but one life to give for his country. And I think of the pain and sadness on the face of Abraham Lincoln, who understood that in order for the nation to free itself from the terrible burden and sin of slavery, hundreds of thousands of young men must die, and that he must oversee their deaths. And I think of the dignified and pacific face of Rosa Parks as she confronts the bullying policeman on the bus. I think that in many ways these are the noble faces of America herself. These are the faces of our best self, the America that God intended—not America as she always is, but America as she was meant to be from the beginning and, by God's amazing grace, will one day become.

There was the Statue of Liberty, as she had been for 115 years, still standing and still offering her torch. But it was more than her dignity in the face of the evil she had recently seen. It was the love. There's no other word for it. I think of a dog that's been kicked and abused by its master but still leaps up and greets that master at the door, even licking his face. Why does that break our hearts? There's something about a love that keeps loving, even in the face of mistreatment and evil. It's the biblical word *agape*. It's not romantic love, which is *eros*, nor friendship love, which is *storge*. It's the love of God, a love that loves even though it is not reciprocated. It is a love that simply gives and gives, and in so doing it breaks our hearts. We even saw it in the firefighters with their heavy gear, marching into the towers that morning, up and up and up as everyone else was racing down and out and away. It is a picture of goodness and it breaks our hearts every time. And that's what I saw that morning when I saw Lady Liberty holding out her torch after all that had happened right there on the southern tip of Manhattan Island, so close to her that if she were alive she could have touched it. After all that had happened to America she was still there, saying: *Welcome. We want you. You are why we are here. You are America. You who are not yet Americans. You are our future. Come.* There she was, still standing and still holding out her torch.

I know that for those immigrants like my own mother and father, she represented America. She *was* America, the bright hope of the world for millions like them. The cynicism we often have about life in general and about our country was nowhere to be found in these countless immigrants like my parents who beheld her from ships entering New York Harbor, who beheld her after suffering and hoping that someday—someday—they might be able themselves to go to that country where they wouldn't be told what to think or how to live or even whether or how to worship. Once they saw her, they knew they were home. Seeing her at last, they didn't roll their eyes and think of the ways America had failed to live up to her noble promises. They thought instead of the promise, and they knew that it was real and that it was promised to them. The promise of liberty the statue represented was not a pious lie people told one another with a wink and a nudge. No. It was true.

My mother told me that after a stormy passage in early April

1954 she was one morning awakened very, very early by the crew of the MS *Stockholm*,[1] who knocked on the door of her tiny, windowless cabin deep in the bowels of the ship. She remembers that it was about five a.m., and she and her cabinmate and everyone else excitedly made their way up, up to the deck and daylight—and suddenly there she was, the fabled statue they had heard about and seen pictures of, and now they could see the real thing. When I asked her what it was like, with a faraway look she said: "It was very emotional."

But I knew then that the events of the past months had enabled me to see this statue as she was meant to be seen, and as she had been seen by all those millions who had needed real hope and who had found it in the country she represented and in the ideal of liberty she represented. Most of them, like my mother and my father, would feel the sting of xenophobic bigotry as in the years following their arrival they did their menial jobs busing tables or cleaning other people's houses, but they did not let it get to them and make them bitter and cynical about the country to which they had come. They knew that the resentment of some who had come to these shores before them was not the truth about America. They knew that resentment was only confirmation that what was here was wonderful and worth fighting to keep. They knew that the great idea behind this great country was that they had as much right to be here as anyone did, and they understood that knowing that and reminding themselves of it was important, and they knew that they must never let that knowledge die, that they must pass it on to their children. And they did.

And part of how they did was in the way they lived their lives for their children to see. They would work very hard, despite the difficulties they encountered, both great and small, and they would keep working hard and would pay their bills and by God's grace would stay and become American citizens and would have American children and would raise their children to love this country that had given them these opportunities—and by God's grace they would one day see their children rise to heights that were not possible for them—and when they saw their children reach those heights, they would rejoice and would say: *This is America. This is America. This is why I came here. This is the country that gave me hope when I had no hope and that gave me and my children an opportunity when we had no opportunities. This is America, the country that welcomed me and that told me I could not only live here but could actually be an American, could actually become a full-fledged member of this community of promise in this nation of nations, and that it wasn't too good to be true, no—it wasn't a lie told to gullible people. It was true and I would love it and live it and pass it on to others, who would pass it on so that others like me could see it and come here as I had come here and so their children could have what my children would have.*

When I saw that statue in the harbor there that morning, I knew something I had never really known before in my life: *I knew that I loved America.* I was aware of her faults and of how far she had to go to live up to her promise, but I knew that day that that promise was real, that that promise was who America was in the eyes of God, and I knew that I had been given the grace of a glimpse of that promise that day—more than a glimpse—and I knew that I loved her and that I had at last seen her as the embodiment of a promise being fulfilled every minute, a promise that must continue to be fulfilled, by you and by me and by everyone and anyone who wishes to be a part of this beautiful and noble experiment in history.

So go forth and love America, knowing that if your love is true it will be transmuted one way or another into a love of everything that is good beyond America, which is her golden promise to the world, and the promise that we, you and I, must keep.

ACKNOWLEDGMENTS

This book would not have been possible without the encouragement and enthusiasm of my editor, Brian Tart, who sensed that my original vision of it as a coffee-table book on white-water rafting—and even my subsequent vision of it as a whimsical children's book about "seven skateboarding gnomes"—needed some editorial tweaking, and who felt free to tweak those rough and misguided visions gently but firmly, until it became what you have in your hands now. His extraordinary forbearance with me in bringing this book to fruition while I was also in the midst of a heavy and unexpected daily radio hosting schedule has been a deep encouragement to me, especially through the tougher patches, which, alas, were extended and several. I also wish to thank my dear friend Jill Lamar for so generously introducing me to Brian several years ago. No acknowledgments page I am writing could be half complete without my heartily thanking my chief of staff, Elisa Leberis, for helping me accomplish nearly everything I've been working on in these last three years, not least through her own great encouragement. Her help in so many ways has been genuinely inestimable and invaluable, and without it this book could not exist. Finally, I wish with all my heart to thank my wife, Susanne, and our daughter, Annerose, for their faith and love through it all.

Soli Deo Gloria.

NOTES

Chapter Two: The Golden Triangle of Freedom

1. Os Guinness spoke about this subject and about his book *A Free People's Suicide* at Socrates in the City. That speech may be viewed at www.socratesinthecity.com.

2. See John J. Pitney's article in *The Weekly Standard* titled "The Tocqueville Fraud," November 12, 1995. This explains the history behind the misattribution of the quote to Tocqueville.

3. For further reading on Jefferson's faith, I recommend *Doubting Thomas: The Religious Life and Legacy of Thomas Jefferson* by Mark Beliles and Jerry Newcombe.

Chapter Four: Venerating Our Heroes

1. The house, built in 1738, still stands at what is today 36 Hancock Street, a National Historic Landmark.

2. See http://www.paulreveresride.org/2010/04/story-of-paul-reveres-ride-part-1.html.

3. Actually, it was a more recently built steeple; the original had blown down in a storm in 1804.

Chapter Six: "The Almost Chosen People"

1. When the poem was written, Brooklyn was still a separate city from New York City.

Epilogue: This Is America

1. This is the ship that two years later would collide with the *Andrea Doria* in one of the greatest maritime disasters of modern times.

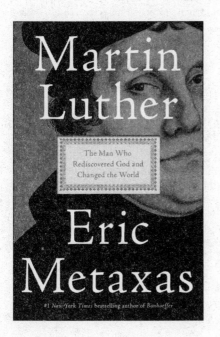

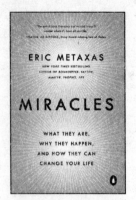

MIRACLES
What They Are, Why They Happen, and How They Can Change Your Life

In this groundbreaking work, Metaxas examines the compatibility between faith and science and provides inspirational stories of actual miracles. Metaxas asserts that miracles are not only possible but are far more widespread than we have ever imagined.

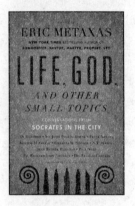

LIFE, GOD, AND OTHER SMALL TOPICS
Conversations from Socrates in the City

First presented to standing-room-only crowds in New York City, these original essays grapple with extraordinary topics from "Making Sense out of Suffering" to "Belief in God in an Age of Science." No question is too big—in fact, the bigger the better—because nowhere is it written that *finding* answers to life's biggest questions shouldn't be exciting and even fun.